Prayers _for_ Victory _in_ Spiritual Warfare

TONY EVANS

HARVEST HOUSE PUBLISHERS
EUGENE, OREGON

Cover by Knail, Salem, Oregon

Cover illustration © iStockphoto / MandarineTree

PRAYERS FOR VICTORY IN SPIRITUAL WARFARE
Copyright © 2015 Tony Evans
Published by Harvest House Publishers
Eugene, Oregon 97402
www.harvesthousepublishers.com

Library of Congress Cataloging-in-Publication Data
    Evans, Tony
    Prayers for victory in spiritual warfare / Tony Evans.
        pages cm
    ISBN 978-0-7369-6058-8 (pbk.)
    ISBN 978-0-7369-6059-5 (eBook)
    1. Prayers. 2. Prayer—Christianity. 3. Spiritual warfare. 4. Spiritual life—Christianity. I. Title.
    BV260.E93 2015
    242'.8—dc23

                                                                    2015015147

Printed in the United States of America
            15 16 17 18 19 20 21 22 23 / BP-JH / 10 9 8 7 6 5 4 3 2 1

Dedicated to the prayer ministry of
Oak Cliff Bible Fellowship,
the unsung heroes of our church.
Thank you for your commitment
in doing battle in the spiritual realm
on behalf of so many in our body.

CONTENTS

FOREWORD

by Priscilla Shirer

My dad, Dr. Tony Evans, is a man of prayer, plain and simple. My childhood memories of his praying are deeply ingrained—hearing his voice resonate with fervor and passion as he lifted up his requests and thanksgiving to God. Not just once a week on Sunday as he led the congregation. No, my father prayed as a lifestyle. He'd gather my siblings and me and our mom, ask us to bow our heads and close our eyes, and then, *then*, he'd talk to God. I admit sometimes I'd peek, opening my eyes just enough to peer up into his face. That's when I *knew*. I knew for sure this discipline was not one he took lightly. His expression was tender and yet serious, compassionate and yet somehow still intent and purposeful. He didn't just pick the usual words and phrases that most easily came to mind. He wasn't hurried or rushed, hoping to quickly return to more important endeavors. This *was* the important task. And as a result of his belief in the power of prayer, I saw God's answers and responses. His Spirit-filled prayer life encouraged our faith as a family and has helped to shape my own personal prayer life as an adult. I'm grateful to call this godly man my pastor...and my father. Grateful, too, that he's sharing some of his wisdom with you in this important book.

In *Prayers for Victory in Spiritual Warfare*, Dr. Tony Evans gives you a jump start in praying for the various needs in your life. In each of the 30 topics covered, he provides you with prayers based on the six pieces of armor outlined in Ephesians 6:10-17. You can pray these prayers verbatim, paraphrase them, or simply let them provoke your thoughts as you craft your own prayers related to these 30 topics—or any other topics you wish to add. The key, however, is to pray. Like my daddy did and still does. Don't just think about prayer, talk about prayer, or learn about prayer. *Actually pray.* Our great God is looking forward to hearing from you and me as we seek His face for victory in the battles we are fighting in our lives.

I will be joining you in claiming the spiritual victory that is ours because we are already more than conquerors in Him who loved us and gave Himself for us. And as you pray, remember that no matter the struggle you are facing, greater is He who is in you than he who is in the world.

Sincerely,

Priscilla Shirer

INTRODUCTION

If you're a Christian, you're in a battle whether you realize it or not. The battle is for your mind, your spirit, and ultimately your life. The apostle Paul warned us about this ongoing conflict in several of his epistles but perhaps most importantly in his letter to the believers in Ephesus, where he also spells out our strategy for winning the battle. That strategy has to do with the armor we wear as we enter into warfare with the enemy of our souls.

> Take up the full armor of God, so that you will be able to resist in the evil day, and having done everything, to stand firm. Stand firm therefore, having girded your loins with [put on the belt of] truth, and having put on the breastplate of righteousness, and having shod your feet with the preparation of the gospel of peace; in addition to all, taking up the shield of faith with which you will be able to extinguish all the flaming arrows of the evil one. And take the helmet of salvation, and the sword of the Spirit, which is the word of God.
>
> With all prayer and petition pray at all times in the Spirit, and with this in view, be on the alert with all perseverance and petition for all the saints (Ephesians 6:13-18).

In my previous book *Victory in Spiritual Warfare*, I wrote extensively on how we're to engage the enemy with our armor in place. Now, in *Prayers for Victory in Spiritual Warfare*, I'm offering some powerful prayers that address some of the major battles we face. For each of the topics listed, you'll find prayers based on each piece of our armor. Because there are six pieces of armor, I've chosen to draft prayers based on the theme of each piece. Feel free to pray the prayers word for word, to use them as a starting point for crafting your own prayers, or to simply paraphrase them. The main thing is that you pray.

My goal is that these prayers will act as a starting place for you each day and that when the prayer I've written ends, you will go on praying in your own words about your situation. Remember as you pray that you do not pray as a beggar, but as a warrior for the King of kings. If you need help discovering what I mean by that and how critical it is that you approach prayer in a sense that you are claiming your legal rights, listen to my online sermon on the subject at go.tonyevans.org/prayer. You have power in prayer over your enemy. You probably have more power than you realize. Your task is to stand firm in your God-given authority, and you do that through prayer. Before you begin, let's take a brief look at each piece of armor.

Armor You Wear All the Time

The first three pieces of the armor of God are to be worn all the time. The "to be" verb—translated "having"—indicates "at all times." You need to be well dressed for warfare every day because the enemy attacks without warning. We are to always put on the belt of truth, the breastplate of righteousness, and the shoes of the gospel of peace.

The Belt of Truth

Wearing the belt of truth involves realizing that truth is fundamentally God-based knowledge—His viewpoint on a matter. These three principles help us put on the belt of truth.

1. Truth is comprised of information and facts, but it also includes God's original intent, making it the absolute, objective standard by which reality is measured.

2. Truth has already been predetermined by God.

3. Truth must be accepted internally and then acted on externally.

When you wear the belt of truth and use it by aligning your mind, will, and emotions underneath God's view on a matter—His truth— He will empower you to overcome the lies of the enemy and fight your spiritual battles with divinely authorized spiritual authority.

The Breastplate of Righteousness

The breastplate of righteousness has already been given to us. Our job is to wear it and use it with the truth of God so that it surrounds us with the protection in warfare we so desperately need.

When you got saved, God deposited deep within you a new heart containing all the righteousness that belongs to Jesus Christ. Righteousness is the standard that pleases God. But you can't benefit from its restoring abilities unless you're willing to dig down with the shovel of truth so that God will release in your decisions and actions a brand-new you, surrounded by the secure protection of the breastplate of His righteousness.

Wearing the breastplate of righteousness involves walking securely in your imputed righteousness by virtue of the cross, coming clean with God in your practice of righteousness, and feeding your spirit with the Word of God so that the Spirit will produce the natural outgrowth of right living from within you.

The Shoes of Peace

A Roman soldier's shoes were called *caliga*—sandals studded heavily with nails. These nails, known as hobnails, were firmly placed directly through the sole of the shoe for increased durability, stability, and traction. This kept the soldier from slipping and sliding, much like cleats help a football or soccer player today. It gave him sure footing, making mobility in battle easier while also making it more difficult to be knocked down.

So when Paul instructs you to have your feet shod, he is talking about placing yourself in a stationary position to stand firm. This creates traction so that when Satan comes, he can't knock you off your feet. In fact, you are able to stand firm because the nails coming out of your "peace shoes" have dug deep into the solid ground beneath you. Paul is telling us that we don't have to slide or move with every hit or trial that comes our way. Having our feet shod with the preparation of the gospel of peace creates a stability that even Satan cannot undo.

God offers us a peace that reaches beyond what we can comprehend. When we receive and walk in that peace, it settles in as a guard over our hearts and our minds. This is the peace that cradles people who lost their jobs so that they don't also lose their minds. This is the peace that produces praise when there is no money in the bank. This is the peace that restores hope in the face of failing health. This peace is so powerful that we're instructed to let it control us. We are taught to let it call the shots, make the decisions, and dictate our emotions.

Putting on peace shoes means aligning your soul under the rule of your spirit. When you choose to do that, God will release peace into your life because the peace of Christ is now ruling your thoughts and actions. When worry creeps back in, you remind yourself that it's lying to you because God has promised that He will provide.

Every attack on peace in your life needs to be taken straight back to the spiritual realm and countered with God's truth on the matter. When you do that, you will wear shoes unlike any others. You will wear shoes that remind the spiritual realm, yourself, and others that you are covered by God's armor. You will walk without becoming weary, and in those shoes you will find the calming power of peace.

Armor to "Take Up" When You Need It

You are to have the next three pieces of armor at hand, ready to pick up and use when you need them. Paul switches verbs for the next three pieces of the armor, telling us to "take up" the shield of faith, the helmet of salvation, and the sword of the Spirit.

The Shield of Faith

Faith is critical to achieving victory in spiritual warfare.

Faith accesses what God has already done or what God plans to do. The shield of faith can also be called the shield that *is* faith because the shield is made up of faith itself.

The Scripture is full of verses that speak to this weapon of faith and where we are to find it. Hebrews 12:2 tells us that Jesus is the "author and perfecter of faith." In Galatians 2:20, Paul explained that he lived by faith in Christ: "I have been crucified with Christ; and it is no longer I who live, but Christ lives in me; and the life which I now live in the flesh I live by faith in the Son of God, who loved me and gave Himself up for me." First John 5:4 says, "For whatever is born of God overcomes the world; and this is the victory that has overcome the world—our faith."

Faith is a powerful weapon, rooted in Jesus Christ. Jesus embodies all the ingredients of faith, from its creation to its perfection. The key to winning in warfare is this faith.

I define faith in practical terms like this: Faith is acting like God is telling the truth. Another way of saying it is that faith is acting like something *is* so even when it is *not* so in order that it might *be* so simply because God *said* so. Your faith must always be directly tied to an *action* done in response to a revealed truth—otherwise, it is not faith. If you are not willing to *do* something in response to the truth—even something as small as simply being still in your soul rather than worrying—then the faith you claim to have is not real. Faith always involves your walk, not just your talk.

Keep in mind, though, that the shield of faith is not just faith in anything. It must be faith in God's truth. Faith is only as valuable as the thing to which it is tied.

For example, if your faith is tied to your feelings—how much faith you feel—your faith will be empty. You might feel entirely full of faith but take no actions in response to that faith because you really don't believe in what you say you feel. True faith is always based on your feet—what you do in response to what you believe. Faith is a function of the mind that shows up in your reactions, responses, and choices to life.

The shield of faith has been given to us to protect us from the deceptive strategies of the enemy. When you use it properly, this shield will enable you to advance against the enemy because you will be confident that what God has said about your situation—in His Word and through His promises—is true.

Pick up the shield of faith, and with it, grab the victory that has already been gained.

The Helmet of Salvation

With the helmet, Paul has once again used a physical example to illustrate a spiritual truth. He demonstrates that just as the brain is the control center for the rest of the body, the mind is the control center for the will and emotions. The mind must be protected with a helmet that's able to absorb the shocks of being hit by the enemy and even knocked to the ground in the spiritual realm.

One reason God wants us to wear a helmet is that the enemy is trying to stop us from accomplishing the things God has for us to do. God wants to speak truth into our minds. He is above all things—seated in the heavenly places—and views the scene below. He can see the field of life much better than we ever could. He can examine the opposition's strategy much better than we can. He has studied the game film much longer than we have. And because of all this, God has a few secrets He wants us to hear. They are secrets because often what God has to say to you is meant only for you.

Satan wants to keep us from wearing the helmet of salvation so that what he whispers to us through his own headset becomes the reality through which we interpret and respond to life.

Everything God is ever going to do for you has already been done. Every healing He will ever give you in your physical body has already been provided. Every opportunity He is ever going to open up for you has already been opened. Every stronghold God is ever going to break in you has already been broken. Every victory you are ever going to experience has already been won. The joy you're desperately seeking already exists. The peace that you stay up at night praying and wishing that you could enjoy is already present. Even the power you need to live the life God has created you to live is already yours. This is because God has already deposited in the heavenly realm "every spiritual blessing" you will ever need (Ephesians 1:3).

Wearing the helmet of salvation means living in that reality now, securely.

The Sword of the Spirit

This piece of armor stands out from all of the others. It's unique because it's the only offensive weapon in the arsenal. Everything else is designed to hold us steady from what the enemy is seeking to bring against us "in the evil day." But after God outfits you for battle in order to stand firm, He gives you an additional weapon with which you can attack and advance.

When Paul instructs us to take up the sword of the Spirit, he's letting us know that in this battle, the enemy will sometimes seem to be close—in fact, right in our face. This can be compared to an opponent trying to block a shot in a basketball game. The opposing player will often stick his body, face, or hands in the offensive player's face so that the offensive player will become disoriented and unable to advance. Satan doesn't want you or me to send the ball through the net for two points, so to discourage this, he brings his battle—your particular stronghold—as close to you as possible. Oftentimes, that means your battle is being waged within you—in your mind, will, emotions, and body.

Paul tells us that this is the sword *of the Spirit*. It's not your sword. It's not the church's sword. It's not the sword of good works or even religion. It's not the preacher's sword. This is the sword of the Spirit, and in fact, it's the only weapon we're told that the Spirit uses in the spiritual realm.

When you learn how to use the sword of the Spirit—which is the Word of God—as you go on the offensive against the enemy seeking to destroy you, it doesn't matter how old you are or how weak you seem. All you need to know is that the sword in your hand is capable of doing more than you will ever need. As Jesus demonstrated in the wilderness, using the sword of the Spirit means communicating to the enemy specific Scriptures that relate to your unique situation.

The Battle in the Heavenlies

Paul ends his discussion on the armor of God with a clarion call to prayer (Ephesians 6:18). Why? Because prayer is how you get dressed for warfare. Prayer is how you put on the armor. I define prayer as relational communication with God. It is earthly permission for heavenly interference. The reason why prayer often seems difficult to us is because Satan seeks to direct us away from it. He knows how important it is. He will use every possible avenue to keep you from seriously communicating with God because he knows what prayer does—it activates heaven's response on your behalf in accordance with the will of God. Prayer does not force God to do what is not His will, but it does release from God to us what *is* His will. And it is definitely His will for His people to wage victorious spiritual warfare.

We find one of the greatest illustrations of prayer in the book of Daniel. Daniel has been studying God's Word, and now he responds to God in prayer based on what he has discovered.

> In the first year of his [Darius's] reign, I, Daniel, observed in the books the number of the years which was revealed as the word of the LORD to Jeremiah the prophet for the completion of the desolations of Jerusalem, namely, seventy years. So I gave my attention to the Lord God to seek

Him by prayer and supplications, with fasting, sackcloth and ashes (Daniel 9:2-3).

First Daniel heard the truth of God. Then he talked to God about it. Anytime you talk with God about His Word, you are praying. You don't have to do it on your knees. You can do it while you are working, hanging out with others, washing dishes…whatever. Prayer in your private room is critical, but try not to neglect the ongoing need for prayer throughout the day as well. Notice what happens next.

> Now while I was speaking and praying, and confessing my sin and the sin of my people Israel, and presenting my supplication before the LORD my God in behalf of the holy mountain of my God, while I was still speaking in prayer, then the man Gabriel, whom I had seen in the vision previously, came to me in my extreme weariness about the time of the evening offering. He gave me instruction and talked with me and said, "O Daniel, I have now come forth to give you insight with understanding" (Daniel 9:20-22).

While Daniel prayed, God responded. He sent an angel to help him understand his situation even more. Notice that God did not send the angel to give Daniel understanding *until* Daniel prayed in response to what God had already said. We read, "At the beginning of your supplications the command was issued, and I have come to tell you, for you are highly esteemed; so give heed to the message and gain understanding of the vision" (verse 23). When Daniel began to pray, God gave Gabriel the directive to go to Daniel to give him more understanding.

The following chapter gives us greater insight into this occasion.

> Then behold, a hand touched me and set me trembling on my hands and knees. He said to me, "O Daniel, man of high esteem, understand the words that I am about to tell you and stand upright, for I have now been sent to you." And when he had spoken this word to me, I stood

up trembling. Then he said to me, "Do not be afraid, Daniel, for from the first day that you set your heart on understanding this and on humbling yourself before your God, your words were heard, and I have come in response to your words. But the prince of the kingdom of Persia was withstanding me for twenty-one days; then behold, Michael, one of the chief princes, came to help me, for I had been left there with the kings of Persia. Now I have come to give you an understanding of what will happen to your people in the latter days, for the vision pertains to the days yet future."

When he had spoken to me according to these words, I turned my face toward the ground and became speechless (Daniel 10:10-15).

When Daniel prayed to God in response to God's words revealed through Jeremiah, God sent a messenger to help Daniel. Twice we read in these two chapters that God sent the angel on the day that Daniel prayed to God with regard to God's already revealed words. When you are praying according to God's own words, He hears you and responds. The delay in receiving that response was due to spiritual warfare in the heavenly realm. Gabriel had been dispatched to go to Daniel with a message of understanding from God, but the prince of Persia—a demon—blocked Gabriel from reaching his destination for three weeks.

Your battle is fought in the spiritual realm. You must not fail to realize that. If you do, you will not fight for the win. As we have seen, when Daniel first offered his prayer, God heard it and responded immediately. Yet because there is a battle taking place in the invisible, spiritual realm, there was a delay in God's response reaching its intended destination. In fact, another angel—Michael—was needed in order to eventually remove the demon from acting as an obstacle for Gabriel. Ultimately, the prince of Persia was double-teamed so God could deliver His message to Daniel.

Rarely is a battle overturned and won in a minute. That is why I want to encourage you to continue in prayer. You may not receive God's response immediately because battles are taking place in the heavenlies.

Taken individually, each piece of armor has a specific use in our warfare against Satan. Taken all together, they present a mighty defense and offense against his tactics. As you pray the prayers on the following pages that are relevant to your needs, my hope is that you'll develop the fighting spirit that warriors need to win the battle and that you will join the mighty army God is raising up as overcomers. Your part in carrying out spiritual warfare can change the course of history for you, your family, your church, your community...even your nation.

1

RECEIVING THE POWER
OF THE HOLY SPIRIT

Walk by the Spirit, and you will not
carry out the desire of the flesh.

GALATIANS 5:16

Have you ever been to a gas station to fill up your car? I imagine you have. One thing you know for sure—when you fill up your car, the gas is not going to last forever. Eventually, the fuel gauge on your dashboard is going to remind you that you are nearing empty and you need to find a gas station again. If you want to continue driving your car, you must keep gas in the tank. No gas, no trip.

Many believers today don't realize that even though we received the Holy Spirit when we trusted in Christ for salvation from our sins, the ongoing dwelling of the Holy Spirit's presence is something we need to seek on a regular basis. Just as driving your car is difficult if it's running on fumes, living the victorious Christian life is impossible without the flame of the Spirit burning bright.

So how do you fill yourself with the Spirit's presence? There are a number of ways. One is to regularly acknowledge and confess your sin because the Holy Spirit is holy and does not dwell intimately in the presence of sin. Another way is by reading God's Word and singing spiritual songs and psalms. Praying and meditating on the character and attributes of God, keeping your mind set on truth, engaging in an atmosphere of communication and communion with God...these things draw you into His presence.

Walk by the Spirit, and you will fully live out the plan God has for you. But remember—to walk by the Spirit, you need to intentionally remain tethered to Him.

Put On the Belt of Truth

Dear Lord, You remind me, "But when He, the Spirit of truth, comes, He will guide you into all the truth" [John 16:13]. So many voices and perspectives surround me—coming from friends, the media, or even my own thoughts—that seek to compete with or counter Your truth. I realize that my history and the things I have experienced may sometimes cloud what I believe to be true. Please let Your Holy Spirit guide me each and every day into all truth. Guide my thoughts and my decisions. Reveal to me where I am thinking wrong. Correct me where I have gotten off track. And grant me the grace to apply the truth You show me through the Spirit to my words and actions so that I reflect Your image more fully in all I do. In Christ's name, amen.

Put On the Breastplate of Righteousness

Father, Your Word tells me that You have "made us competent to be ministers of a new covenant, not of the letter but of the Spirit; for the letter kills, but the Spirit gives life" [2 Corinthians 3:6]. The law is not my righteousness because on my own, even on my best day, I can only claim like Paul that I am unrighteous [Romans 3:10]. Give me the grace to live according to the newness of the Spirit, pleasing You in all that I do, and may I do this out of a heart filled with gratitude for all You have done for me. In Christ's name, amen.

Put On the Shoes of Peace

Lord, one of the evidences of a Spirit-filled life is peace [Galatians 5:22]. You have given me the Holy Spirit so I can speak to the chaos around me or in me just as Jesus spoke to the storm on the sea, "Be still." Thank You, God, for empowering me to wear the shoes of peace. Holy Spirit, I pray I may know and be protected by Your peace—peace that passes comprehension [Philippians 4:7]—so that I will respond calmly when other people disappoint me or when circumstances seem to be against me. In Christ's name, amen.

Take Up the Shield of Faith

Dear God, in times of doubting, fear, or anxiety, I might try to turn to a crutch to get me through that moment or that day. Whatever that crutch is, Lord, if it is not faith in You, I am choosing to fill myself with something other than Your Holy Spirit. Help me in those times to remember that I have access to Your presence and the Spirit's power. Remind me to whisper a simple prayer, turning my thoughts to You, and not to seek something else to cover my fears and doubts or distract me from them. In Christ's name, amen.

Take the Helmet of Salvation

Lord, I am secure. I am secure because of the work of Christ on the cross and because He sent the Holy Spirit to remain with me all of my days on earth. I thank You that whatever I face, nothing will separate me from Your love. The Holy Spirit is a constant reminder of that promise. I bless Your name because "there is therefore now no condemnation for those who are in Christ Jesus. For the law of the Spirit of life in Christ Jesus has set [me] free from the law of sin and death" [Romans 8:1-2]. I want to live as if I believe that fully, Lord. Take my guilt and hesitation over things I have done wrong so that I may boldly walk in the confidence of my relationship with You. In Christ's name, amen.

Take Up the Sword of the Spirit

Lord, as I take up the sword of the Spirit today, give me wisdom through Your Word to align my thoughts, words, and actions under You. Where I am struggling, Lord, direct me to Scriptures that reveal the truth so I can apply it to my own mind and repel Satan's attacks. Jesus, You used the Word of God when Satan tempted You in the desert. You countered Satan's lies with the truth by saying, "It is written…" and then proclaiming the truth. Show me where I have been duped by the devil, and guide me to the correlating truth to counteract it in each of these areas I am bringing to You in prayer. In Christ's name, amen.

Victory

Pray and ask God to reveal any of your misguided thoughts, beliefs, or words about the Holy Spirit or your relationship to the Spirit. Ask Him to show you how you have tried to cope with difficulties in life instead of turning to the filling of the Spirit. For each untruth, look for a countering truth from God's Word. When you write down the countering truth, be sure to cross out the untruth and pray, in Christ's name, that it will no longer affect your life and the lives of those around you. Then thank God that the power of His truth has been let loose to do its work of healing, empowerment, and grace in you. Here's an example.

- *Untruth*: I have coped with pain through [overspending, drinking, yelling…] for so long, I could never stop it now.
- *Truth*: "If anyone is in Christ, he is a new creature; the old things passed away; behold, new things have come" (2 Corinthians 5:17).

2

MAINTAINING A SPIRITUAL PERSPECTIVE

*Set your minds on the things above, not
on the things that are on earth.*

Colossians 3:2

Victory in spiritual warfare comes down to one foundational thing—your perspective. What are you looking at? Are you staring at whatever is right in front of you? Or are you looking from the perspective of the heavenly places? Unless you learn to operate from up there, you will succumb to your challenges down here.

The enemy's nature and the way he operates his opposing kingdom make it essential that you learn to think and live from a spiritual mindset. Why? Because if you don't, it will be as if you are trying to fight a land battle in Ohio from Alaska. You can strategize all you want in Alaska, and even equip yourself to wage war, but your strategies and your weapons will not be effective simply because you aren't able to accurately size up the enemy from afar. And when it comes time to wage war, you will be too far away to accomplish anything at all.

Similarly, unless you keep your mind set on spiritual things, you won't recognize Satan's agenda when you see it, and you won't be able to wage victorious spiritual warfare.

You need to learn to put the spiritual ahead of the physical because your real battle is against a spiritual kingdom that seeks to dominate you spiritually. Satan knows that if he can get your mind, he can dictate your actions. To wage victorious warfare in the heavenly places, you must set your mind on Christ and His truth.

Put On the Belt of Truth

Dear Lord, Your Word tells me where I am spiritually. "Even when we were dead in our transgressions, [God] made us alive together with Christ (by grace you have been saved), and raised us up with Him, and seated us with Him in the heavenly places in Christ Jesus" [Ephesians 2:5-6]. I am seated with You in the heavenly places. That means Your authority and power have been made available to me through the death and resurrection of Jesus Christ. "When [Jesus] had disarmed the rulers and authorities, He made a public display of them, having triumphed over them through Him" [Colossians 2:15]. You have already secured my victory. Help me to remember this when I feel attacked or defeated. I am not fighting *for* victory, Lord, I am fighting *from* victory. In Christ's name, amen.

Put On the Breastplate of Righteousness

Father, my righteousness is in Christ. I have great worth and value because of Christ's supreme worth and value. Satan may tempt me to doubt these things, but I believe Your Word.

> Therefore as you have received Christ Jesus the Lord, so walk in Him, having been firmly rooted and now being built up in Him and established in the faith, as you were instructed, and overflowing with gratitude.

> See to it that no one takes you captive through philosophy and empty deception, according to the tradition of men, according to the elementary principles of the world, rather than according to Christ. For in Him all the fullness of Deity dwells in bodily form, and in Him you have been

made complete, and He is the head over all rule and authority [Colossians 2:6-10].

I am to walk in Christ with all of the confidence that His purity,
cleanness, and righteousness grant me. I am complete in Christ because
of His victory over all principalities and powers. No one trumps Jesus.
In Christ's name, amen.

Put On the Shoes of Peace

Lord, peace is often hard to come by, especially in the middle of a battle. When I see chaos around me, I get afraid. I get concerned about the
future. Or if a relationship, my finances, my health—anything—seems
to be crumbling or burning, I can worry at times. You have given me a
kingdom truth in Your Word to apply to times like these: "You keep him
in perfect peace whose mind is stayed on you, because he trusts in you"
[Isaiah 26:3 ESV]. I don't have to create my own internal peace. I don't
have to try to force it when I am feeling shaken. All I have to do is set
my mind above in the heavenly places—set it on You and Your power,
provision, purpose, and protection. When I do, You have promised me
peace. As peace enters my thoughts, my mind will then guide my feet,
and I will walk in the peace that comes with knowing You've got me. In
Christ's name, amen.

Take Up the Shield of Faith

Dear God, operating from a heavenly mindset and a kingdom perspective requires faith. I must believe that You are the ultimate victor and You
have already defeated Satan. If I don't believe this, I will cower in fear.
Faith gives me all I need to be patient, to not be controlled by my emotions, and to wait on Your timing and deliverance in all things. If I know
the end of something, and that end is good, then I can walk through
the difficulty with confidence, peace, and joy. So by setting my mind on
You, Lord, and on what has been secured for me in the heavenly places,
I accept Your victory as my own. I thank You ahead of time for how You

will bring about my deliverance and my victory against every issue I face in faith. In Christ's name, amen.

Take the Helmet of Salvation

Lord, if Jesus Christ had only died on the cross, I could not count on You. I could not look to Him in the heavenly places. Nor would I be seated with Him there. But I *can* face my spiritual battles with strength because Christ not only died but also rose and ascended to the heavenly places. Because of this, You have granted me understanding into "the mysteries of the kingdom of heaven" [Matthew 13:11]. And to me "God willed to make known what is the riches of the glory of this mystery among the Gentiles, which is Christ in [me], the hope of glory" [Colossians 1:27]. Christ in me is my victory. In Christ's name, amen.

Take Up the Sword of the Spirit

Lord, when Jesus was on earth, He spoke truth and gave us power in His words. In His words—the truth—I find the sword to defeat Satan's schemes and lies. So I choose to follow Your Word:

> Let the word of Christ richly dwell within you, with all wisdom teaching and admonishing one another with psalms and hymns and spiritual songs, singing with thankfulness in your hearts to God. Whatever you do in word or deed, do all in the name of the Lord Jesus, giving thanks through Him to God the Father [Colossians 3:16-17].

When I let the Word of Christ dwell in me, it is the sword that counteracts and defeats the enemy. Help me to know and learn Your Word more and more each day so I can have access to it easily and readily in my thoughts. In Christ's name, amen.

Victory

Pray and ask God to reveal your misguided thoughts, beliefs, or words about the heavenly places, about the location of your enemy and your spiritual battles, and about your role in fighting unwanted circumstances and temptations in your life. For each untruth, look for a countering truth from God's Word. When you write down the countering truth, be sure to cross out the untruth and pray, in Christ's name, that it will no longer affect your life or the lives of those around you. Then thank God that the power of His truth has been let loose to do its work of healing, empowerment, and grace in you. Here's an example.

- *Untruth*: My [mate, coworker, family member…] is my enemy.

- *Truth*: "Our struggle is not against flesh and blood, but against the rulers, against the powers, against the world forces of this darkness, against the spiritual forces of wickedness in the heavenly places" (Ephesians 6:12).

3

WINNING WITH THANKS

Be anxious for nothing, but in everything by
prayer and supplication with thanksgiving let
your requests be made known to God.

PHILIPPIANS 4:6

Just like any effective military commander, Satan has a battle plan. One tactic he uses to defeat you is to distract you. He tries to take your focus off the truth and put it on what you see and experience instead. In this way, he tempts you to complain, gripe, or even give up. Satan wants you to do what Eve did in the garden—dismiss the value of what you have been given to enjoy while fixating on what you don't have. He wants you to forget God's many blessings and to focus instead on what you think you lack. Satan tries to divert your gaze from God's goodness because he knows the only way to defeat you is through deception.

Yet God is not fooled by smoke and mirrors or by what you plainly see. He has already won this battle. To enjoy the fruit of His victory, you need to employ a strategy of giving thanks. Had Eve chosen to be grateful for the numerous trees in the garden she could eat from rather than lust for the one she could not, Satan's scheme would not have worked as it did. This is because a complaining spirit kills in a variety of ways—mainly by promoting envy and wrong desires. This takes away our ability to experience God's promised abundant life. We may experience this in the death of a dream, relationship, career, virtue, or any number of other things.

Like water on the wicked witch in *The Wizard of Oz*, gratitude and thanksgiving destroy Satan's influence. Use this weapon wisely and frequently to enjoy the victory that is yours.

Put On the Belt of Truth

Dear Lord, Your Word tells me not to be anxious, but instead to give thanks. And You don't stop there. You go on to say that if I will obey You and align my heart and mind with Your kingdom principle of giving thanks, I will enjoy many blessings.

> The peace of God, which surpasses all understanding, will guard your hearts and minds in Christ Jesus.

> Finally, brethren, whatever things are true, whatever things are noble, whatever things are just, whatever things are pure, whatever things are lovely, whatever things are of good report, if there is any virtue and if there is anything praiseworthy—meditate on these things. The things which you learned and received and heard and saw in me, these do, and the God of peace will be with you [Philippians 4:7-9 NKJV].

In giving thanks and thinking on good things rather than complaining, I will experience both the peace of God and the God of peace. I will have a double return on what I do. Thank You, God. In Christ's name, amen.

Put On the Breastplate of Righteousness

Father, when I give thanks to You, I am responding to what You have done. I am placing my faith in Your goodness and trusting in Your sovereign wisdom over all. Although things may not look fine in every area of my life, I always have something to thank You for—the fact that I am still here, or that You still have a plan for me, or that You always provide for me…

> Both riches and honor come from you, and you rule over all.
> In your hand are power and might, and in your hand it is to
> make great and to give strength to all. And now we thank
> you, our God, and praise your glorious name.
>
> But who am I, and what is my people, that we should be able
> thus to offer willingly? For all things come from you, and of
> your own have we given you [1 Chronicles 29:12-14 ESV].

All things come from You, and every ounce of strength I have is a gift from You. Even my ability and heart's desire to thank You is a result of Your inner prompting in my spirit. Thank You, God, for receiving my thanksgiving—who am I that I should even be able to offer it to You? My gratitude comes from You, so please give me more of You so that I can give more back to You. In Christ's name, amen.

Put On the Shoes of Peace

Lord, it is easy to give thanks in times of blessing and security. But Your Word tells me to give thanks in times when I would rather worry or be anxious. When Daniel faced a serious difficulty and a decree had been made against those who worshipped You, he did not cower in fear or become combative to those who had enacted it. Neither did he complain to You about allowing him to be in a situation like that. Instead, Daniel sought peace by giving thanks.

> When Daniel knew that the document had been signed, he
> went to his house where he had windows in his upper cham-
> ber open toward Jerusalem. He got down on his knees three
> times a day and prayed and gave thanks before his God, as
> he had done previously [Daniel 6:10 ESV].

Help me to seek peace in my own heart and in my relationships by giving thanks in seasons and situations that would normally cause me to complain. In Christ's name, amen.

Take Up the Shield of Faith

Dear God, giving thanks in times of anxiety and fear is one of the greatest steps of faith I can take. In periods of lack or loss, I naturally want to complain, just as the Israelites did in the desert for so many years. To give thanks is to say directly to Satan that I trust in You, God, and Your goodness. I have faith that You will bring about my deliverance and victory despite how things appear. You did not tell me to give thanks *for* all things—You told me to give thanks *in* all things [Philippians 4:6]. I can do that. I can thank You in the middle of a mess because I know You can turn a mess into a miracle. There is a lot to thank You for when I realize I am giving thanks *in* a situation rather than *for* it. I can thank You for being above all rule and authority and for defeating Satan. I can thank You for hearing my prayers. I can thank You for loving me despite my failures and sins. Thank You, God, for calling me to a higher level of faith through giving thanks. In Christ's name, amen.

Take the Helmet of Salvation

Lord, thank You for making my victory secure. Thank You for not letting anything separate me from You.

> In all these things we overwhelmingly conquer through Him who loved us. For I am convinced that neither death, nor life, nor angels, nor principalities, nor things present, nor things to come, nor powers, nor height, nor depth, nor any other created thing, will be able to separate us from the love of God, which is in Christ Jesus our Lord [Romans 8:37-39].

Even though the circumstances I find myself in can look shaky on many levels, and even though I may let myself down in how I respond, I know that Your grace covers my sin and gives me another opportunity to give You thanks. In Christ's name, amen.

Take Up the Sword of the Spirit

Lord, when I give You thanks, I am being obedient to Your Word. Your Word says, "Give thanks in all circumstances; for this is the will of God in Christ Jesus for you" [1 Thessalonians 5:18 ESV], and "Whatever you do, in word or deed, do everything in the name of the Lord Jesus, giving thanks to God the Father through him" [Colossians 3:17 ESV]. Satan no longer has victory over me because I have chosen the strategy of gratitude to You. I will not sin against a good and gracious God by complaining. Instead, I give You thanks even when I cannot understand and even when things seem to be different from what I want. I thank You because I trust You and Your ways are higher than mine. You have a bigger picture of what is truly going on. I am going to trust in Your vantage point rather than my own by giving You thanks even in times that cause me pain. In Christ's name, amen.

Victory

Pray and ask God to reveal any of your thoughts, beliefs, or words in which you have been complaining, grumbling, doubting, or questioning. For each example of ingratitude, look for a countering truth from God's Word. When you write down the countering truth, be sure to cross out the unhelpful attitude and pray, in Christ's name, that it will no longer affect your life and the lives of those around you. Then thank God that the power of His truth has been let loose to do its work of healing, empowerment, and grace in you. Here's an example.

- *Untruth*: I do not have everything I need to be truly happy and satisfied.

- *Truth*: "God is able to make all grace abound to you, so that always having all sufficiency in everything, you may have an abundance for every good deed" (2 Corinthians 9:8).

4

THE AUTHORITY OF CHRIST

He rescued us from the domain of darkness, and
transferred us to the kingdom of His beloved Son, in
whom we have redemption, the forgiveness of sins.

COLOSSIANS 1:13-14

When Jesus Christ died on the cross, He made it possible for you to be complete in Him and in His rule, which extends over everything. "In Him you have been made complete, and He is the head over all rule and authority" (Colossians 2:10). No lack exists in Jesus Christ. Because He is complete, you are complete in Him. His headship and His rulership extend over all.

How would you act if a stranger on the street pointed a gun at you? Would your heart race? Would you freeze, or would you run? Now, how would you act if that same stranger pointed a gun at you, but you knew the gun was not loaded? It's a whole different ball game then, isn't it? In spiritual warfare, Satan likes to wave his gun at you from a lot of angles. But your victory is rooted in the truth that Christ removed the bullets. The gun is empty. Christ rendered Satan powerless through His death.

Since the children share in flesh and blood, He Himself likewise also partook of the same, that through death He might render powerless him who had the power of death, that is, the devil, and might free those who through fear of death were subject to slavery all their lives (Hebrews 2:14-15).

In Jesus Christ, you have been set free and no longer have to cower in fear. Your victory is rooted in the reality that everything is under the One who has made you complete in Him. When you trusted in Christ for your salvation, you were transferred from the dominion of darkness into the victorious kingdom of light.

Put On the Belt of Truth

Father, I praise You for giving all authority to Jesus Christ. Your Word says, "He put all things in subjection under His feet, and gave Him as head over all things to the church, which is His body, the fullness of Him who fills all in all" [Ephesians 1:22-23]. As a member of Christ's church, His body, I represent the fullness of Him who fills all in all. I have complete and total access to the greatest authority over all. Nothing can stand in my way when I seek Jesus Christ and His power in faith and humility. He holds the keys that unlock the power to bind the gates of hell from advancing on my mind, relationships, future, career, and all other things. Satan wants me to forget that truth. My emotions do not dictate the truth. How I feel at any given moment does not dictate what is true. The truth is that all things have been put in subjection under Jesus's feet. I am in Christ, so His authority is always available to me as I live aligned under Him. Thank You for this. In Christ's name, amen.

Put On the Breastplate of Righteousness

Lord, I am righteous in You because of Jesus Christ. Christ has in fact become my righteousness, and righteousness has become my breastplate in the war against the enemy. I claim Christ's righteousness and His victory as my own, not because of any righteous thing I have done, but because I have placed my faith in Him. Satan keeps whispering to me that I am righteous in my own flesh, but that's a lie, and I refute it and replace it with the truth of God's Word. My victory does not come out of my own goodness. Rather, I will boast in my weakness because when I am weak, Christ in me is strong. In Christ's name, amen.

Put On the Shoes of Peace

Today, Lord, I wear the shoes of peace, shoes especially fit for me as pieces of my armor against Satan. These shoes lead me on the path You've designed especially for me. This path is mine alone, carved out for me by Your hand. You have created me for this path and given me authority in Christ that can overcome all opposition. I praise You and thank You for Your individual attention and care for me. I praise You and thank You that just as Jesus stood and calmed the waves of the storm with only His words, He has authority to calm any storm in my life when I call on Him. Jesus is my source of peace because Jesus has authority over chaos. In Christ's name, amen.

Take Up the Shield of Faith

Father, I take up the shield of faith to combat the lies the enemy throws at me—lies that I am powerless, fearful, weak, defeated, and so much more. In truth, I am able to overcome any scheme of the devil when I place myself under the authority of Jesus Christ. When I put my faith in His authority, He will fight and win my battles for me. Placing my faith in His authority, though, also means that I don't turn to my own methods to fight as well. Faith is complete and total trust, so I let go of my ways, Lord, and look to You to carry out the victory in the way You choose. I trust that You will guide me with all wisdom, revealing the part I am to play in each battle I face. In Christ's name, amen.

Take the Helmet of Salvation

Lord, at my salvation, You made me a new creation [2 Corinthians 5:17]. I praise You for this great salvation, which gave me authority through Jesus Christ. Satan, I am a saved and redeemed person. I am no longer a citizen in your kingdom. Rather, I am a citizen in God's dominion of light and truth. God's salvation equips me with every tool to overcome your tactics and your accusations. Lord, thank You for this, my helmet of salvation. In Christ's name, amen.

Take Up the Sword of the Spirit

Lord, Your sword is able to stop Satan in his tracks because it is truth. The authority given to Jesus Christ has not rendered Satan powerless. He still has power, but that power can be cancelled through Your authority. Help me remember that Satan still has power so that I don't seek to fight him with my own power. I would not win that battle. I win only when I face Satan with the authority of Jesus Christ. So I must abide in Christ and let His Word abide in me so that I will always have my sword handy to overcome the schemes of the devil. Thank You for giving me this wisdom. In Christ's name, amen.

Victory

Pray and ask God to show you any of your thoughts, beliefs, or words that reveal a heart of defeat or fear. Also consider anything you have thought or said that would be considered giving up in the battle against the enemy. For each of these negative examples, look for a countering truth from God's Word. When you write down the countering truth, be sure to cross out the untruth and pray, in Christ's name, that it will no longer affect your life and the lives of those around you. Then thank God that the power of His truth has been let loose to do its work of healing, empowerment, and grace in you. Here's an example.

- *Untruth*: Satan always knows the right buttons to push to get me to respond or react the wrong way.

- *Truth*: "No temptation has overtaken you but such as is common to man; and God is faithful, who will not allow you to be tempted beyond what you are able, but with the temptation will provide the way of escape also, so that you will be able to endure it" (1 Corinthians 10:13).

5

VICTORY IN MARRIAGE

Marriage is to be held in honor among all.

HEBREWS 13:4

God created marriage with a purpose in mind—a mission. A kingdom marriage isn't solely about making you happy or making your spouse happy. A kingdom marriage successfully merges mission with emotion. Far too often, though, couples will lose sight of the mission and purpose, and they will focus on the disappointment of unmet expectations regarding their emotions. Then when happiness fades or the spark fizzles, they think that their marriage is over, or their disappointment leads to conflict and complaining.

God created Adam and Eve to exercise dominion. He said, "Let them rule" (Genesis 1:26). To exercise dominion is to rule on God's behalf in history so that history comes underneath God's authority. Simply put, the mission of marriage is to replicate God's image in history and to carry out His divinely mandated dominion. I go deeper into the dominion mandate in my teachings on marriage, but for the purposes of your prayers, know that the Lord has brought the two of you together in order to reflect His image on earth in the most holistic manner possible—through the union of man and wife. He is advancing His heavenly authority and rule on earth through your spheres of influence.

Happiness is a wonderful benefit of a strong marriage, but it's not the goal. The goal is the reflection of God through the advancement of His kingdom on earth. Happiness occurs as an organic outgrowth when you first seek this goal. If you are not married, apply these prayers to your future spouse. Or if you intend to never marry, pray for a married couple you know and love.

Put On the Belt of Truth

Lord, the foundation of any healthy marriage is love. Not love as the world defines it, made up only of emotions of attraction or desire. Nor is it frivolous, as when I say, "I love chocolate cake." Maintaining a committed, marital love is the hardest and yet most strategic thing I can do for my marriage. It requires me to take my eyes off my spouse and my expectations for him/her to satisfy me, and it places my eyes squarely on myself and what I am giving or how I am responding. You have defined this love:

> Love is patient and kind; love does not envy or boast; it is
> not arrogant or rude. It does not insist on its own way; it is
> not irritable or resentful; it does not rejoice at wrongdoing,
> but rejoices with the truth. Love bears all things, believes all
> things, hopes all things, endures all things [1 Corinthians
> 13:4-7 esv].

Living that kind of love would make any marriage strong, Lord. So I pray that my heart will truly embody the character of love that You desire it to have. In Christ's name, amen.

Put On the Breastplate of Righteousness

Father, Your Word tells us, "There is none righteous, not even one" [Romans 3:10]. Neither I nor my spouse is righteous, and we definitely are not perfect. I look to You, Lord, to perfect us in the many areas where we need to grow. As You perfect us, help us to remember that we will never fully be perfect and to give each other grace for our weaknesses and imperfections. Help us to view each other through lovers' kind, caring, and patient eyes. Help us to not look to each other to meet all our needs. Only Christ is perfect, and only He can meet all our needs perfectly. In Christ's name, amen.

Put On the Shoes of Peace

Lord, You know there are issues and areas in my marriage that could drive my spouse and me apart. But God, I ask You, in the name of Jesus our Lord, to heal these areas and bring peace to our home and our hearts. Lord, start with me. Help me put on the shoes of peace when I'm with my spouse. Let me reflect Your peace when I respond to misunderstandings or conflict. And Satan, in the name of Jesus, I rebuke and bind your attempts to disrupt the peace of God in our home and in our hearts. I declare our home and our marriage a place of peace, calm, and mutual kindness. In Christ's name, amen.

Take Up the Shield of Faith

Lord, I lift my spouse to You today and pray, according to Your Word, that my spouse would love You with all of his/her heart, soul, mind, and strength [Mark 12:30]. I have faith that if I pray for my spouse according to Your Word, You hear me, and I have the answers to my prayers. I also pray that my spouse will be quick to hear, slow to speak, and slow to anger [James 1:19]. Guide my spouse in the path to take [Psalm 32:8], and help my spouse to make decisions with integrity [2 Corinthians 8:21]. In faith, I pray that my spouse will remain faithful to You at all times [Hebrews 12:1-2]. Because I am praying according to Your Word, I know I have the things for which I am asking even though I don't know how You will bring them about. Help me to let go and make room for You to work in my spouse's life even when I don't understand Your methods. In Christ's name, amen.

Take the Helmet of Salvation

Father, You know the lies the enemy has spoken over our marriage. I have sometimes listened to those lies and even believed them, but now I repent. God, I put on Your helmet of salvation—Your saving power—and I listen to You and Your Word regarding my marriage. Satan, in the name of Jesus Christ, I will no longer listen to your accusations and lies about my marriage. What God has joined together, you cannot separate. In fact, what God has joined together, no one can separate, not even ourselves, when we live in the light of His truth. In Christ's name, amen.

Take Up the Sword of the Spirit

I praise You, Father, for Your Word, which is the sword of the Spirit. By this sword, I go on the offensive against Satan and his deceiving attempts to ruin my marriage. In Jesus's name, I pierce the lying tongue of the enemy with the truth that "He who finds a wife finds a good thing and obtains favor from the Lord" [Proverbs 18:22]. His every lie is brought to nothing with the truth that "a man shall leave his father and mother and hold fast to his wife, and the two shall become one flesh" [Ephesians 5:31 ESV]. Satan's every evil accusation is dispelled with the truth that "steadfast love and faithfulness meet; righteousness and peace kiss each other" [Psalm 85:10 ESV] in my marriage. Lord, I rejoice and praise You for fully equipping me with every piece of armor I need to overcome the enemy so I can live in a fully victorious kingdom marriage. In Christ's name, amen.

Victory

Pray and ask God to reveal your negative thoughts, beliefs, or words about your marriage, your spouse, or yourself as a partner. Also consider anything you have thought or said that goes against God's values for marriage or His purpose for marriage. Ask Him to remind you of things you have said directly to your spouse that are not based on biblical love. For each of these negative examples, look for a countering truth from God's Word. When you write down the countering truth, be sure to cross out the untruth and pray, in Christ's name, that it will no longer affect your life and the lives of those around you. Then thank God that the power of His truth has been let loose to do its work of healing, empowerment, and grace in you. Here's an example.

- *Untruth*: My spouse doesn't treat me with respect, and I'm afraid I will be left alone either emotionally or physically.

- *Truth* (believe this characterizes your marriage): "Love one another with brotherly affection. Outdo one another in showing honor" (Romans 12:10 ESV).

6

OVERCOMING FEAR AND ANXIETY

Do not fear, for I am with you;
Do not anxiously look about you, for I am your God.
I will strengthen you, surely I will help you,
Surely I will uphold you with My righteous right hand.

ISAIAH 41:10

Shortly before Jesus was crucified, He gave a powerful example of overcoming what should have produced fear and anxiety. Jesus knew what was going to take place. He knew He was about to go into a very chaotic and painful situation. Yet in the middle of it all, He told His disciples, "Peace I leave with you; My peace I give to you; not as the world gives do I give to you. Do not let your heart be troubled, nor let it be fearful" (John 14:27). Jesus was saying that His peace is different from the world's peace. He was letting His disciples in on a very important principle—that despite the troubling situation about to occur, they did not need to be troubled or afraid because His peace was greater than anything they had ever known.

The world might offer you peace in a pill, a song, a drink, a relationship, a Louis Vuitton bag...the world serves up peace in a variety of ways. But the world's peace is a cheap imitation of God's peace.

God's peace produces rest on the inside. It remains. God's peace triumphs over fear and anxiety because God's peace comes from Christ Himself. And Christ is the same yesterday, today, and tomorrow—nothing rattles Him. No matter what is going on around you—even if it's a cross—you do not need to be afraid. You may not like it, but you can handle it because Christ can handle it and He gives you full access to His peace. As Jesus said, "These things I have spoken to you, so that in Me you may have peace. In the world you have tribulation, but take courage; I have overcome the world" (John 16:33).

Put On the Belt of Truth

Lord, the only fear I need is the fear of You. In truth, the fear of God is the beginning of wisdom. To reverence You in fear means to take You seriously. To take You seriously means to align my thoughts and actions in accordance with who You are and Your comprehensive rule over all. I walk in the knowledge that Your truth brings freedom from fear and anxiety, but the enemy's lies feed my fears—even when there is actually nothing to fear. Peace is found in Jesus Christ, so as I abide in Him, His peace is manifest in my spirit, thoughts, and choices. I overcome fear and anxiety by deepening my dependence on and intimacy with Jesus Christ my Lord. In His name, amen.

Put On the Breastplate of Righteousness

Lord, sometimes I experience fear and anxiety because I distrust Your goodness and because of my unrighteousness. I'm not perfect, and I've done and said things that I'm not proud of. When these thoughts linger in my mind, I don't count on Your protection, provision, and peace as much as I should. Instead of going boldly to Your throne of grace, I go timidly because I don't always feel worthy to be in Your presence. Yet Your promise of peace in my life is not based on my righteousness. It's based on the righteousness of Jesus Christ, secured for me on the cross. His peace is to be my peace. Thank You, Lord. In Christ's name, amen.

Put On the Shoes of Peace

Lord, the psalmist wrote, "When I am afraid, I will put my trust in You" [Psalm 56:3]. When I trust in You, You exchange my fears for Your peace. I put on the shoes of peace by trusting in Your presence and power, knowing that it is my job to seek You in the midst of my fear and anxiety. "I sought the LORD, and he answered me, and delivered me from all my fears" [Psalm 34:4]. I also put on the shoes of peace by humbling myself. I recognize my inadequacy and my lack of control. Much of fear stems from a need for control, but ultimately I do not control anything. Being anxious on an airplane does not keep it in the sky. Being fearful of ill health does not keep me healthy. Being afraid that my marriage or relationships will deteriorate does not keep them strong. This is because ultimate control is in Your hands, and no matter what happens, You use it for good when I love You. Humility allows me to acknowledge that You know better than I do. "Humble yourselves, therefore, under the mighty hand of God so that at the proper time he may exalt you, casting all your anxieties on him, because he cares for you" [1 Peter 5:6-7 ESV]. In Christ's name, amen.

Take Up the Shield of Faith

Lord, faith and fear cannot coexist in one mind. So I choose faith over fear. I raise the shield of faith against every fearful or anxious thought from the enemy. Through Christ, I have the power to do this. Satan, you must yield to the shield of faith. You may no longer instill fear or anxiety in my mind, in Jesus's name. I proclaim myself free from your fearsome taunts because I am in Christ and Christ is peace. In Jesus's name, amen.

Take the Helmet of Salvation

Father, sometimes my mind wanders back to my old fears and anxieties, but with Your helmet of salvation, I can ward off those thoughts and accept Your thoughts of peace, joy, and love. Satan, I rebuke your unholy thoughts that cause me to fear that which can do me no harm because of my trust in Christ. My helmet of salvation is strong against your fearful thoughts. In Christ's name, amen.

Take Up the Sword of the Spirit

O Lord, thank You for the sword of the Spirit! Thank You that I can slay every fearful and anxious thought or temptation of the enemy with this weapon. I will not be anxious about my life, because You care for the birds of the air, and I am more valuable than they are [Matthew 6:26]. Your love for me is perfect—"There is no fear in love; but perfect love casts out fear" [1 John 4:18]. Your love casts out my fears because I can trust You. When I feel anxiety arising in my thoughts, I will cast my anxiety on Christ because He cares for me [1 Peter 5:7]. In Christ's name, amen.

Victory

Pray and ask God to reveal your fearful or anxious thoughts, beliefs, or words. Also consider anything you have thought or said that questions God's promise of peace. Or even things you have said directly to others that do not reflect a heart of trust in God. For each untruth, look for a countering truth from God's Word. When you write down the countering truth, be sure to cross out the untruth and pray, in Christ's name, that it will no longer affect your life and the lives of those around you. Then thank God that the power of His truth has been let loose to do its work of healing, empowerment, and grace in you. Here's an example.

- *Untruth*: I am afraid of what might happen in this situation.

- *Truth*: "Do not worry about tomorrow, for tomorrow will care for itself. Each day has enough trouble of its own" (Matthew 6:34).

7

HEALING BROKEN RELATIONSHIPS

…bearing with one another, and forgiving each
other, whoever has a complaint against anyone;
just as the Lord forgave you, so also should you.

CoLossians 3:13

The emotional pain of a broken relationship is as hard to bear as physical pain—sometimes even worse. And as with physical pain, healing must be sought. Jesus Christ can identify with our pain because He experienced rejection firsthand (John 1:11). Part of the warfare for healing a broken relationship is believing God can heal your emotions. When God heals your emotions, you can be sure that memories of the broken relationship, thoughts about how it broke, and other triggers won't send you into a tailspin.

In some situations, relationships can be healed and the people can be reunited. Other relationships may not be reconciled, and in those cases you will need to seek healing from the broken relationship itself. Whatever the case you find yourself in, carrying around emotional pain is similar to living with an untreated wound. It can lead to further infections as the bacteria of bitterness and regret is left to spread.

Imagine having an open wound on your arm (hidden under your shirt). Someone brushes up against you, unaware of your wound. You suddenly jerk your arm and perhaps become angry, say something unkind, or walk away in pain. These reactions don't make sense to the person who accidentally brushed up against you. You appear to be overreacting.

Overreactions are tied to old reactions that have not yet healed.

That is why it is critical to either heal your broken relationship with someone or be healed from the broken relationship itself. Otherwise, you run the risk of letting past wounds harm your future relationships.

Put On the Belt of Truth

Lord, I know that life goes on after a relationship is broken. In fact, the truth is that You're the one who moves us on when the time is right or a relationship is unhealthy and toxic. Still, it's painful. I pray You will give me strength to walk through this new truth in my life and come out in a better place. Or if it is Your will for our relationship to be restored, I pray that You will give us both the grace we need to restore it well. I put on the belt of truth that tells me, "In all things God works for the good of those who love him, who have been called according to his purpose" [Romans 8:28 NIV]. In Christ's name, amen.

Put On the Breastplate of Righteousness

Father, today, I put on the breastplate of righteousness. I know the enemy would try to use my broken relationship to discourage me or accuse me. But with my breastplate guarding my heart, I stand firmly against this tactic of Satan. I made mistakes in this relationship, Lord. I did or said things that were wrong, even if it was just my bitter reactions to the other person. Satan wants to remind me of my guilt and to tell me I'm not good enough to keep a relationship intact. But You, God, are my righteousness. In You I am made whole. I take comfort in knowing the truth that in You, I am good enough and forgiven from all wrong. Help me to show that same grace to those around me who need my forgiveness and acceptance. In Christ's name, amen.

Put On the Shoes of Peace

Today, Lord, I thank You that I can put on the shoes of peace and walk in forgiveness in the aftermath of this broken relationship. When I'm tempted to doubt or to despair over the break, please remind me that Your ways are the ways of peace and that by wearing these shoes as part of my armor against the enemy, I can continue in undisturbed peace. No relationship ends peacefully, simply because of the pain of tearing apart what was once valued. Lord, Your Spirit provides perfect peace, so if You are willing to restore peace to this relationship, I pray that You will. Help my words and thoughts about this person and our relationship to be filled with peace from this point forward. In Christ's name, amen.

Take Up the Shield of Faith

God, You are the author of my faith. Today I need my faith to act as a shield in the ongoing struggle with this broken relationship. May the darts of the enemy fall to the ground as I trust in this resilient shield. By faith, I will walk through this pain and heal from the hurt. I have faith that You can redeem that which I believed was lost. I have faith that You can restore our love, affection, and kindness for one another. If You so choose, Lord, You can bind our broken hearts in a deeper unity than before. Yet if You choose not to, You can also heal us on our own. In faith, Lord, I thank You for bringing about healing from this pain and loss. In Christ's name, amen.

Take the Helmet of Salvation

Father, today I put on the helmet of salvation and reject every thought or painful memory that drags me down. In the name of Jesus Christ, I rebuke the enemy and his lies about the other person in this broken relationship. He must be silenced as I trust in the pure and peaceful thoughts that come from above. Every painful episode in my life can be turned to gold when I trust in You. You have the power to teach me through this struggle so that I become a kinder person whose love is purer than ever before. Protect my current and future relationships as well by helping me apply the lessons I've learned from this broken one, Lord. And thank You that no matter what I've done to You in the past, You have never left me. In Christ's name, amen.

Take Up the Sword of the Spirit

Lord, by the mighty sword of the Spirit, I take every negative thought captive. I cast down imaginations that cause me to remember how this broken relationship used to mean so much to me. I also cast down thoughts of how it has hurt my self-esteem. Your truth tells me, "The LORD is the One who will go before you. He will be with you; He will not leave you or forsake you. Do not be afraid or discouraged" [Deuteronomy 31:8 HCSB]. After experiencing a broken relationship, it is easy to transfer those fears to others, Lord—even to You. So thank You for the confidence I have in Your Word, which says, "He Himself has said, 'I will never desert you, nor will I ever forsake you'" [Hebrews 13:5]. Nothing can separate me from You, Lord, or from Your love [Romans 8:31-39]. Thank You for this assurance. And please fill my heart with Your joy, which is my strength [Nehemiah 8:10]. In Christ's name, amen.

Victory

Pray and ask God to bring to the surface the destructive thoughts, beliefs, or words you may have had or spoken when this relationship was breaking apart. Maybe they are words you said to the other person about yourself or about him/her. Also ask God to reveal any effects this has had in your beliefs about yourself—your own esteem, value, security, and worth. For each untruth, look for a countering truth from God's Word. When you write down the countering truth, be sure to cross out the untruth and pray, in Christ's name, that it will no longer affect your life and the lives of those around you. Then thank God that the power of His truth has been let loose to do its work of healing, empowerment, and grace in you. Here's an example.

- *Untruth*: I am not worth loving.

- *Truth*: "The LORD your God is in your midst, a mighty one who will save; he will rejoice over you with gladness; he will quiet you by his love; he will exult over you with loud singing" (Zephaniah 3:17).

8

LETTING GO OF UNFORGIVENESS

*Be kind to one another, tender-hearted,
forgiving each other, just as God in
Christ also has forgiven you.*

EPHESIANS 4:32

How do you climb a mountain? One step at a time. Overcoming unforgiveness is a lot like that. It's a long process with small victories along the way. You may feel as if you have forgiven someone or yourself, only to have a trigger bring to the surface those same raw emotions of anger, bitterness, fear, and regret. I want to encourage you—in those times, don't give up, but keep going step-by-step. Carrying unforgiveness with you throughout your life will affect you in more ways than you realize.

Just as a disease can spread in your body, the effects of unforgiveness can spread from your painful relationships and infect your healthy ones. Keeping friends becomes more difficult. Small offenses get blown out of proportion. You begin to withhold love and generosity to protect yourself from being hurt again. For these reasons and many more, it is critical that you learn to forgive.

Biblical forgiveness is the decision to no longer credit offenses against others. You choose not to take vengeance. You release them from the debt they owe. You no longer blame them for what they did to you.

The best biblical defense for this definition of forgiveness is found in 1 Corinthians 13, where we read about love. In verse 5 we discover that love "keeps no record of wrongs" (NIV). This is similar to how God forgives us. He doesn't forget the sin, but He no longer holds the offense against our account. He doesn't require us to pay a debt we are unable to pay.

Put On the Belt of Truth

Thank You, Lord, for forgiving me. I put on the belt of truth, which tells me that You don't hold any of my sins against me or even choose to remember them. Any suggestion of unforgiven sin is a lie from the enemy, and in Jesus's name, I refuse to accept it. Likewise, I choose to forgive those who have hurt me in any way. I choose to release them from any grudge or bitterness I've harbored against them. And where my emotions don't yet follow, Lord, I ask You for an extra measure of grace to help me let go of this anger and bitterness. Forgiveness is a choice based on Your love. Thank You for modeling what that looks like in my own life. In Christ's name, amen.

Put On the Breastplate of Righteousness

Lord, today I put on the breastplate of righteousness as a protection against unforgiveness. Regardless of the offense, I refuse to allow the unrighteousness of unforgiveness to cloud my walk with You or to break my fellowship with You. I am not perfect, but when I know I am doing wrong, Lord, I want Your help to do right. I have been hurt. In fact, I can still feel the pain and disappointment. But I ask for Your healing to come quickly. Please bind up my wounds so I won't add more pain to my life through unrighteous choices prompted by unforgiveness. In Christ's name, amen.

Put On the Shoes of Peace

Thank You, God, for the shoes of peace. When I wear these shoes, I walk in peace with all people, even those who have offended me. I put on the shoes of peace as a weapon against the bitter consequences of unforgiveness. I stand firm in my willingness to completely forgive those who have hurt me, just as You have forgiven me. God, when I disrupt someone else's life by not forgiving him/her, I disrupt my life as well, and I no longer walk in Your shoes of peace. Forgive me, Father, for choosing pain over peace in those times. Please save me from the error of my ways. In Christ's name, amen.

Take Up the Shield of Faith

Father God, when the enemy reminds me of someone who has hurt me—tempting me to replay that experience over and over in my head, causing those old feelings of anger to rise in my heart—I rebuke him in Jesus's name. Satan, I dash every one of your bitter reminders to the ground because of the shed blood of Christ. You have no authority to keep reminding me of real or perceived hurts. I am choosing to trust God in faith to use for my good what someone else meant for harm [Genesis 50:20]. In Christ's name, amen.

Take the Helmet of Salvation

Lord, I guard my mind from memories of past hurts by putting on Your helmet of salvation. I choose to dwell on thoughts of forgiveness and reconciliation. Satan, in the name of Jesus Christ, I refuse your evil thoughts of anger, revenge, and hate. The feelings you attempt to raise in me are toxic, and I will not accept them. Lord, I pray for those who have offended me. I ask You to bring blessing and healing into their lives. And if there is any evil intent in their hearts, I pray You'd show them their sin and release them from their bondage. In Christ's name, amen.

Take Up the Sword of the Spirit

Heavenly Father, I take up the sword of the Spirit in my battle to completely forgive. I repent of any feelings of bitterness. I lay aside any desire to get even. I pray for You to bless those who have offended me, for Your Word says, "I say to you, love your enemies and pray for those who persecute you" [Matthew 5:44]. And Satan, in the name of Jesus, I take the sword of the Spirit, which is the Word of God, and I slash your every evil reminder of my pain and every temptation to be angry with someone. I receive God's Word, which instructs me to be kind, patient, humble, and not easily angered [1 Corinthians 13]. It is in His truth that I will set my hope for victory. In Christ's name, amen.

Victory

Pray and ask God to remind you of any of your thoughts, beliefs, or words that reveal a spirit of unforgiveness. Also try to discern areas where you feel you deserve to hold on to your anger. I also want you to think of areas where you may not yet have truly accepted God's forgiveness in your own life. Write these all down. For each untruth, look for a countering truth from God's Word. When you write down the countering truth, be sure to cross out the untruth and pray, in Christ's name, that it will no longer affect your life and the lives of those around you. Then thank God that the power of His truth has been let loose to do its work of healing, empowerment, and grace in you. Here's an example.

- *Untruth*: My pain justifies my anger.
- *Truth*: "If anyone has caused grief, he has not so much grieved me as he has grieved all of you to some extent—not to put it too severely. The punishment inflicted on him by the majority is sufficient. Now instead, you ought to forgive and comfort him, so that he will not be overwhelmed by excessive sorrow. I urge you, therefore, to reaffirm your love for him" (2 Corinthians 2:5-8 NIV).

9

USING MY SPIRITUAL GIFTS

One and the same Spirit works all these things,
distributing to each one individually just as He wills.

1 CORINTHIANS 12:11

One of the greatest treasures you can find as a follower of Jesus Christ is your spiritual gifts. A spiritual gift is a divinely bestowed ability that strengthens the body of Christ and serves the kingdom.

A spiritual gift is much different from a talent. It is something uniquely given and enhanced by God to service His people and His agenda for the expansion of His kingdom. We call them spiritual gifts because they are given by the Holy Spirit and used through the power of the Holy Spirit for God's purposes. Have you ever seen someone who was highly talented but whose talent didn't make any real, lasting impact? On the other hand, have you ever seen someone who may not have been the most talented but who seemed to bless everyone around them?

A spiritual gift may be something you didn't know you could do before you became a believer. Oftentimes people discover their spiritual gifts when they develop a relationship with the Holy Spirit.

Many Christians fail to maximize their calling simply because they are not aware of their spiritual gifts. They may be stuck trying to utilize a talent rather than seeking God for the gifts He has given them or discovering how God wants to transform a talent into a gift. Other Christians fail to maximize their calling because they don't even know they have spiritual gifts. If you are a believer in Jesus Christ, you have at least one spiritual gift. God has equipped you with the necessary skills to fulfill the destiny for which you were created. God never calls you to do something He does not equally provide for. God always prepares you for His unique purpose for you.

Put On the Belt of Truth

Thank You, Lord, for the spiritual gifts You have given to me. I know You have given them to me because You have a plan for me, and it is a good plan [Jeremiah 29:11]. You knew me before You formed me in the womb, and then You created me to fulfill Your purpose in my life [Jeremiah 1:5]. Lord, Satan would like nothing more than to derail me from Your calling and destiny for me, so he creates doubts in my mind about my abilities, purpose, or usefulness to You. I reject those doubts in Jesus's name because I believe the truth of Your Word, which says, "It is God who is at work in you, both to will and to work for His good pleasure" [Philippians 2:13]. In Christ's name, amen.

Put On the Breastplate of Righteousness

Lord, it's easy to look around at other people and compare myself with them. It's easy to feel as if You would rather use someone else to advance Your kingdom instead of me, and to see their gifts as more strategic than mine. These are also lies from Satan. You have gifted me for a unique purpose that is perfectly adapted to my background, personality, passions, and skills. Thank You for my spiritual gifts. I trust that You have chosen to use me not because of my righteousness but because of the righteousness of Christ Jesus in me. I believe You can use me as a powerful tool in Your hands to bring good to the lost and hurting around me. In Christ's name, amen.

Put On the Shoes of Peace

Thank You, Lord, that I can walk in peace when I embrace the truth of Your calling and purpose in my life. Lord, Satan seeks to derail me from my service in Your kingdom, and one way he does that is by stirring up conflict in the areas where You desire to use me. It's easy to run from conflict in order to seek peace—to run from the storm—but that would give Satan victory. Satan wants me to leave the area of my spiritual gifts. But I look to You, Lord, to give me calm in the chaos when I am serving You. Keep me in the heart of my purpose, and give me peace in the midst of opposition. I trust in You, Lord. In Christ's name, amen.

Take Up the Shield of Faith

Father God, You have promised, "Whatever you ask in prayer, you will receive, if you have faith" [Matthew 21:22 ESV]. With this shield, I ask You to maximize my spiritual gifts for Your kingdom. I ask You to place a hedge of protection around me to ward off Satan's attempts to get me off course from doing and being all You have created me to do and be. I ask You to reveal to me any spiritual gifts that I do not yet recognize, and also to sharpen and refine my spiritual gifts for their greatest use. In Christ's name, amen.

Take the Helmet of Salvation

Lord, I am secure through Jesus Christ, who gave His life for me. Thank You that I do not need to worry or wonder about my value or purpose because You have already established both. My spiritual gifts are secure as well, and I want You to use them to their fullest. I know I will find my greatest joy in living a life of purpose. I trust my purpose carries with it eternal rewards because of what Christ did for me on the cross. Thank You for that. In Christ's name, amen.

Take Up the Sword of the Spirit

Heavenly Father, I turn to Your Word, which pierces Satan to the core.

> When I came to you, brethren, I did not come with superiority of speech or of wisdom, proclaiming to you the testimony of God. For I determined to know nothing among you except Jesus Christ, and Him crucified. I was with you in weakness and in fear and in much trembling, and my message and my preaching were not in persuasive words of wisdom, but in demonstration of the Spirit and of power, so that your faith would not rest on the wisdom of men, but on the power of God [1 Corinthians 2:1-5].

I reject any lie of Satan that I have to be the very best at what I do in order for You to use me in a mighty and powerful way. In fact, You can use me most effectively in my areas of weakness because when I depend on You, Your strength comes through. I praise You for Your wisdom, for knowing exactly how You empower me to impact others for good. In Christ's name, amen.

Victory

Pray and ask God to show you any of your thoughts, beliefs, or words that reveal doubt in your usefulness to the kingdom, or hesitation to be used in your areas of spiritual gifting. Also consider any pride you may have about areas of strength. Write these all down. For each untruth, look for a countering truth from God's Word. When you write down the countering truth, be sure to cross out the untruth and pray, in Christ's name, that it will no longer affect your life and the lives of those around you. Then thank God that the power of His truth has been loosed to do its work of healing, empowerment, and grace in you. Here's an example.

- *Untruth*: I am insignificant.
- *Truth*: "Then God said, 'Let us make man in our image, after our likeness. And let them have dominion over the fish of the sea and over the birds of the heavens and over the livestock and over all the earth and over every creeping thing that creeps on the earth'" (Genesis 1:26 ESV).

10

PRAYERS FOR MY HOUSEHOLD

When I saw their fear, I rose and spoke to the nobles,
the officials and the rest of the people: "Do not be
afraid of them; remember the Lord who is great and
awesome, and fight for your brothers, your sons,
your daughters, your wives and your houses."

NEHEMIAH 4:14

Satan has a plan against your home and family. If you are single, he has a plan against you and your future family or your relatives. As our nation continues to turn away from God's intended order, Satan's plan escalates. Just as he issued his plan in the Garden of Eden, Satan has put a plan in place in our nation today. The target is the family because as goes the family, so goes the nation.

If Satan can undermine God's foundation for a strong home, he can cause all manner of chaos, destruction, and devolution in our society. This is because family units are the building blocks of society. Children, future leaders, and contributors to society are created, nurtured, and matured in the family.

Satan's goal is not merely to disrupt and destroy your home. It is to disrupt and destroy your future and the futures of the people in your home. He wants your children to have negative experiences that will hinder them when they have their own families. This way he sets in motion a destructive cycle of dysfunction.

Only when we return to God's design and purpose for the family will we once again enjoy God's blessing on our lives and our nation. When we align our hearts, minds, and purposes under His kingdom agenda and rule, we will experience the full and abundant life Christ died to give.

Too many in the body of Christ today have grown complacent toward the attack on the biblical family. That is exactly where Satan wants you to be. Don't settle for anything less than God's plan for your home, even if that means you have to fight spiritually for it.

Put On the Belt of Truth

Today, Lord, I pray for my family. I put on the belt of truth and establish truth as the foundation of my life, my home, and my loved ones' lives. Guard us, God, from the enemy. Let Your truth prevail in our family in all we do. We refuse to allow the enemy's lies to undermine the work You're doing in us. Your Word says, "Whoever troubles his own household will inherit the wind, and the fool will be servant to the wise of heart" [Proverbs 11:29 ESV]. Lord, lead me in Your truth—I don't want to bring trouble to my family. I carry Your truth with me and ask You to keep me from straying from it. In Christ's name, amen.

Put On the Breastplate of Righteousness

Lord, may ours be a righteous home. May the breastplate of righteousness rebuff any attacks on our home or on members of our family. We forsake any known unrighteousness and accept Your forgiveness. We deny the enemy's access to our home in the name of Jesus Christ. He has no place of entrance as we continue wearing the breastplate of righteousness. We are not perfect, Lord, but You are making us more like You every day. Give us the grace we need to forgive each other fully from the heart. Pour kindness into our hearts so we will encourage each other to live lives of righteousness, hope, and peace. In Christ's name, amen.

Put On the Shoes of Peace

Today I put on the shoes of peace for myself and for my family. I pray the supernatural peace of God would dwell in this home, bringing calm when there is strife. I rebuke the enemy for every attempt to bring chaos and confusion to my family members. I pronounce the peace and blessing of God over my home. I pray, Lord, that You will intervene with a spirit of peace when conflict and hurt begin to boil to the surface. In those moments, before things get out of hand, remind us of Your power and Your provision of peace. In Christ's name, amen.

Take Up the Shield of Faith

Father, You see the many missiles the enemy fires at my family. I praise You for the shield of faith, which I raise up to deflect Satan's every attack on us. In the name of Jesus Christ, I am confident that Satan's poisonous darts are stopped cold when they encounter our shield of faith. God, I know You have a purpose for my family. We are to collectively advance Your kingdom and Your agenda on earth. We are to individually reflect Your heavenly image in our earthly history. By faith, even though we are not perfect, I know we will do just that because this is Your will and this is my prayer, and when those two combine, I know I have victory! In Christ's name, amen.

Take the Helmet of Salvation

Today, Lord, I put on the helmet of salvation to protect my family from the assaults of the enemy. I refuse to hear any false accusation or criticism that would bring division to our household. God, I pray Your special blessing on each and every family member and on our family as a unit. We are committed to You and trust in You for the security You give us. We are living in a culture and time when the family unit is no longer valued, Lord. This can make family members feel insecure on a number of levels, so I trust that You will cover our home with the security of this helmet. In Christ's name, amen.

Take Up the Sword of the Spirit

Dear Lord, the attack on my family is severe. Satan tries to divide us or create chaos when I know You mean for us to be at peace and enjoy Your blessing. I take up the sword of the Spirit—Your Word—and I declare firmly, "As for me and my house, we will serve the LORD" [Joshua 24:15]. I carry Your Word in my heart concerning the power of a kingdom home:

> How blessed is everyone who fears the LORD,
> Who walks in His ways.
> When you shall eat of the fruit of your hands,
> You will be happy and it will be well with you.
> Your wife shall be like a fruitful vine
> Within your house,
> Your children like olive plants
> Around your table.
> Behold, for thus shall the man be blessed
> Who fears the LORD.
> The LORD bless you from Zion,
> And may you see the prosperity of Jerusalem all the days
>   of your life.
> Indeed, may you see your children's children.
> Peace be upon Israel! [Psalm 128].

This is my desire for my home. In Christ's name, amen.

Victory

Pray and ask God to reveal any of your thoughts, beliefs, or words that are not true about the family unit in general or about your family in particular. Also write down any disappointments or issues you may have with other family members. Note any ways you feel as if you have let your family down. Write these all down. For each untruth, look for a countering truth from God's Word. When you write down the countering truth, be sure to cross out the untruth and pray, in Christ's name, that it will no longer affect your life and the lives of those around you. Then thank God that the power of His truth has been let loose to do its work of healing, empowerment, and grace in you. Here's an example.

- *Untruth*: We lack a spiritual focus.

- *Truth*: "If it is disagreeable in your sight to serve the LORD, choose for yourselves today whom you will serve: whether the gods which your fathers served which were beyond the River, or the gods of the Amorites in whose land you are living; but as for me and my house, we will serve the LORD" (Joshua 24:15).

11

LETTING GO OF EMOTIONAL BONDAGE

The thief comes only to steal and kill and destroy;
I came that they may have life, and have it abundantly.

JOHN 10:10

An emotional stronghold isn't the same thing as simply having a bad day. We all have bad days or even bad weeks. An emotional stronghold is an attitude or emotion that stays with you day in and day out. It does more than just show up from time to time. It dictates and dominates your thoughts and choices and thus your life itself.

God never intended for you to wake up depressed every day or to always be paralyzed by fear. He didn't create you to carry anger around for five, fifteen, or fifty years. God has promised you a full life in Christ. If you're not experiencing the abundant life Christ freely gives, you may be living with an emotional stronghold.

God wants to free you from the endless and fruitless task of denying or suppressing emotional strongholds through distractions, pills, entertainment, spending, or the like. He wants to reveal to you the root behind what you are experiencing. Just as a doctor will not only listen to how you feel when you go in for an examination but will also probe deeper through X-rays or tests, so too overcoming emotional strongholds involves going deeper than just your feelings to discover the root cause.

Certainly, some emotional strongholds are tied to physiological causes, such as a chemical imbalance, and those need to be addressed physically. However, a large number of emotional strongholds are not physiological. They are rooted in sin. The sin may be your own, or someone else's sin may be affecting you, or your environment may be contaminated by sin. Maybe you were abused as a child, raped, betrayed in a relationship, or unwanted. It wasn't *your* sin that created the stronghold of fear, insecurity, guilt, or shame that you may be facing now. But it was still sin that caused it.

Emotional strongholds often come as a result of what I call *atmospheric sin*—sin that so clouds the atmosphere around us that its results affect us whether we committed the sin or not. It's similar in concept to secondhand smoke and lung cancer. You may not have smoked the cigarettes yourself, but studies show that if you grew up in a home contaminated by cigarette smoke, you have a higher potential for contracting lung cancer. The same holds true for sin. An environment deeply contaminated by sin leads to a greater susceptibility to emotional strongholds.

Put On the Belt of Truth

I praise You, Lord, for providing healing for my emotions. You created my every emotion for a reason, but when not surrendered to You, my emotions can cause me all sorts of trouble. I thank You for the belt of truth. As I wear it, my emotions are submitting to the truth, aligning with the truth, and following the truth. Your Word says that I can do all things through Christ, who strengthens me [Philippians 4:13], and that Your power is perfected in weakness [2 Corinthians 12:9]. I know I can overcome these emotional strongholds through You. In Christ's name, amen.

Put On the Breastplate of Righteousness

God, I trust in the breastplate of righteousness as I live out my freedom from emotional bondage. In righteousness, there are no traumatic emotional ups and downs—just the unchanging nature of my imputed righteousness giving me victory over fluctuating emotions. Emotions do not have intellect, God; they simply fluctuate according to my circumstances and my surroundings. So I choose instead to set my mind on You and Your righteousness because in You is the fullness of life. "You will make known to me the path of life; in Your presence is fullness of joy; in Your right hand there are pleasures forever" [Psalm 16:11]. In Christ's name, amen.

Put On the Shoes of Peace

I praise You, Father, for the shoes of peace, which give me continued undisturbed emotional freedom when I wear them. With these shoes, I walk daily in the power of Your Spirit and am able to resist every negative emotion Satan throws at me. Lord, help me to stop kicking them off. I need Your peace, especially in times of emotional vulnerability. Remind me of Your peace so I can call on You in times of need. You have offered a wonderful invitation: "Call upon Me in the day of trouble; I shall rescue you, and you will honor Me" [Psalm 50:15]. You promise, "The LORD is near to all who call upon Him, to all who call upon Him in truth" [Psalm 145:18]. Thank You, Lord, that I can trust You to be there for me. In Christ's name, amen.

Take Up the Shield of Faith

God, I rejoice in my shield of faith, which stops every emotionally destructive arrow Satan shoots at me. I hold my shield high, guarding my heart, mind, and soul from depression and every other evil intention of the enemy. In Christ's name, amen.

Take the Helmet of Salvation

Lord, Satan wants to get at my emotions by suggesting depressing thoughts and discouraging imaginations filled with pity and doubt. Therefore, I put on the helmet that guards against his vicious attacks—the helmet of salvation, which saves me emotionally and in every other way. You love me, Lord [John 3:16], and You have a good plan for my life [Jeremiah 29:11]. In Christ's name, amen.

Take Up the Sword of the Spirit

Father, with every attack on my emotions that Satan launches, I take up the Word of God, which is my sword of the Spirit. With that sword, my victory in spiritual warfare for my emotions is guaranteed. Sharpen my sword, Lord. Keep me diligent to wield it at the first notice of every satanic attack on my emotions. Right now I resist Satan with Your Word, which says, "Fear not, for I am with you; be not dismayed, for I am your God; I will strengthen you, I will help you, I will uphold you with my righteous right hand" [Isaiah 41:10 ESV]. And "Have I not commanded you? Be strong and courageous. Do not be frightened, and do not be dismayed, for the LORD your God is with you wherever you go" [Joshua 1:9 ESV]. In Christ's name, amen.

Victory

Pray and ask God to reveal your discouraging thoughts, beliefs, or words; your sentiments of giving up...anything that reflects a spirit of insignificance or anything similar. Also think of things others may have said to you to cause you to believe you were not valuable or were unable to be victorious in your life. Write these all down. For each untruth, look for a countering truth from God's Word. When you write down the countering truth, be sure to cross out the untruth and pray, in Christ's name, that it will no longer affect your life and the lives of those around you. Then thank God that the power of His truth has been let loose to do its work of healing, empowerment, and grace in you. Here's an example.

- *Untruth*: I will never amount to anything.

- *Truth*: "For I know the plans I have for you, declares the LORD, plans for welfare and not for evil, to give you a future and a hope" (Jeremiah 29:11).

12

PRAYERS FOR FAVOR

Let the favor of the Lord our God be upon us;
And confirm for us the work of our hands;
Yes, confirm the work of our hands.

PSALM 90:17

Favor is a powerful thing. Favor gives you good things you don't necessarily deserve. It also gives you what you need to accomplish what you couldn't do on your own. Favor can be given from person to person (Esther 2:17; 5:8; 7:3), from God to people (Genesis 6:8; Psalm 84:11 ESV), or from both (Luke 2:52). Whatever the case, favor is something to pray for on a regular basis.

Nehemiah models this for us. In contemporary terms, he was a beast. He accomplished in 52 days what no one had done for Israel in 141 years. Nehemiah was a dedicated man who turned millions of people's lives around for good through his hard work and commitment—and by receiving favor.

We first find Nehemiah asking for favor in the opening chapter of the book named after him. He is distraught, discouraged, and near despair due to the plight of his people who survived the exile and returned to the province of Jerusalem, only to discover the walls broken down and the gates burned with fire. Nehemiah first sought the Lord, repenting on behalf of himself and his people. Then he took action. He wanted to use his position as the cupbearer to King Artaxerxes to leverage support for his people.

So he asked God for favor. "'Give your servant success today by granting him favor in the presence of this man.' I was cupbearer to the king" (Nehemiah 1:11 NIV). As the story unfolds, we learn that God did indeed give Nehemiah favor with the king, and as a result, Nehemiah was well supplied and protected as he rebuilt the walls of Jerusalem.

But Nehemiah's wise request for favor did not stop there. Multiple times throughout the rest of the book we read things like this: "Remember me with favor, my God, for all I have done for these people" (Nehemiah 5:19 NIV). He even closes the book by praying, "Remember me with favor, my God" (Nehemiah 13:31 NIV). Nehemiah wasn't a perfect man. But he accomplished a lot in his life because he found favor with God and the king. We often forget to ask for favor, and Satan tries to keep us from seeking favor because he doesn't want us to fulfill the calling and purpose God has for us.

What if Nehemiah had tried to rebuild Jerusalem without the king's favor? Would he have been so successful? What if he had tried to restore the spiritual state of his nation without God's favor? Favor is critical, and that's why spiritual warfare includes asking for favor.

Put On the Belt of Truth

The truth is, Lord, that Your favor lasts a lifetime. That is why I want it and ask for it. Your Word says, "His anger is but for a moment, and his favor is for a lifetime. Weeping may tarry for the night, but joy comes with the morning" [Psalm 30:5 ESV]. Just as Abraham prayed in Genesis, I ask right now, "O Lord, if I have found favor in your sight, do not pass by your servant" [Genesis 18:3 ESV]. I ask that I would find favor with You, God, and with others who will be able to help me fulfill the purpose You have for my life. In Christ's name, amen.

Put On the Breastplate of Righteousness

Lord, You tell me in Your Word that I will find favor with You when I live my life with love and righteousness. "Let not steadfast love and faithfulness forsake you; bind them around your neck; write them on the tablet of your heart. So you will find favor and good success in the sight of God and man" [Proverbs 3:3-4 esv]. I want to live with steadfast love and faithfulness. Help me to make decisions and to think thoughts that will help me live with both. Thank You. In Christ's name, amen.

Put On the Shoes of Peace

Thank You, God, that when I walk in peace, Your favor is upon me. "Toward the scorners he is scornful, but to the humble he gives favor" [Proverbs 3:34 esv]. Humility walks in shoes of peace, Lord. I put on this peace because I seek Your favor. Give me favor not only with You but also with my family members, spouse, children, coworkers, and those who can open doors for me in order to accomplish what You have called me to do. When I am in Your presence, I find favor and peace. "The Lord make his face to shine upon you and be gracious to you; the Lord lift up his countenance upon you and give you peace" [Numbers 6:25-26 esv]. In Christ's name, amen.

Take Up the Shield of Faith

Father God, Your favor carries with it a lot of power. It kept Esther alive when she could have been killed. It provided the way for the escaping Israelites to have what they needed when they left Egypt. "I will give this people favor in the sight of the Egyptians; and when you go, you shall not go empty" [Exodus 3:21 esv]. I have faith that whatever I am facing—a rift in a relationship, a financial burden, a health issue, a job situation—if You will grant me favor, I can overcome. Grant this favor, Lord, so that I will receive Your power. In Christ's name, amen.

Take the Helmet of Salvation

Lord, my salvation started with favor. It was granted to a young girl who carried the Christ child in her womb. "And the angel said to her, 'Do not be afraid, Mary, for you have found favor with God'" [Luke 1:30 ESV]. Favor is a powerful thing, God. I ask You for favor in my relationships, on my job, with my finances, and in my health. Most of all, Lord, give me favor with You. In Christ's name, amen.

Take Up the Sword of the Spirit

Heavenly Father, I take up the sword of the Spirit against Satan and say to You, "You are the glory of their strength; by your favor our horn is exalted" [Psalm 89:17 ESV]. I have victory because of Your favor. I also stand against Satan by affirming that I am covered by Your favor. "For you bless the righteous, O LORD; you cover him with favor as with a shield" [Psalm 5:12 ESV]. You are my sun and shield, and You bestow favor and honor [Psalm 84:11]. Thank You for Your favor, God, because it is the key to my victory. In Christ's name, amen.

Victory

Pray and ask God to reveal any of your thoughts, beliefs, or words that show you have been complaining or feeling overwhelmed. Also think of things you may have said that reveal a spirit of giving up in the face of great challenges or fears. In addition, note any insecurity you may have. Write these all down. For each untruth, look for a countering truth from God's Word. When you write down the countering truth, be sure to cross out the untruth and pray, in Christ's name, that it will no longer affect your life and the lives of those around you. Then thank God that the power of His truth has been let loose to do its work of healing, empowerment, and grace in you. Here's an example.

- *Untruth*: I have no control over how somebody views me.
- *Truth*: "Remember me, O Lord, when you show favor to your people; help me when you save them" (Psalm 106:4 ESV).

13

RECOVERING FROM LOSS

Surely our griefs He Himself bore,
And our sorrows He carried.

ISAIAH 53:4

Jesus wept from grief at the death of his friend Lazarus. He was well acquainted with sorrows. Whatever grief or loss we experience, God understands. In fact, the Holy Spirit is also called the Comforter. Surely one of His comforts is peace when we grieve a profound loss. What loss has caused you grief? Take it to the Lord. Don't let your grief become a source of bitterness that gives the enemy a foot in the door.

God longs for a deep and abiding relationship with you. Because He is dependable, He wants you to depend on Him. God can use your sorrows to strengthen your relationship with Him.

If you are healthy, you aren't likely to be going to the doctor's office anytime soon. This is because everything in your body seems to be working and doing what it is supposed to do. But when you become sick, and especially if that sickness continues for a long time, chances are that you will make an appointment to go visit your doctor. You will choose to enter into your doctor's presence.

Similarly, sometimes God allows loss in your life to get your focus back onto Him. He doesn't want you to walk this road alone. He is with you even when you forget that He's there. He longs to be close to you.

Are you in a situation that wants to eat you alive? Are you finding yourself with less and less hope each day? Do you ever feel overwhelmed with regret over what you have lost?

If that describes your situation, then I want nothing more than to remind you that Jesus is with you. He is right there with you right now. And I want you to fully know that because He is with you, His power and His grace are with you. And His power and grace will comfort you.

God sometimes calls us to walk through a valley. I can't promise that life will be without wind, clouds, and rain. But I *can* promise that you don't have to walk through the valley of loss alone. If you will cast your eyes on Jesus Christ, He will meet you where you are. So keep walking. Don't throw in the towel. Don't say that you can't make it, because God will make it with you. You don't walk this road alone.

Put On the Belt of Truth

Father, in my loss, I feel unstable, shaken. I pray that You will sustain me as I put on the belt of truth. Thank You for being with me even in my darkest sorrow. Lord, I pray the enemy would not gain a foothold through this devastating loss. God, please help me so that this loss doesn't create in me a root of bitterness that Satan can use to take me down the wrong path [Hebrews 12:15]. I don't want this loss, Lord, but I have to trust that You are a good God who chooses and allows what is best for me, even in this. In Christ's name, amen.

Put On the Breastplate of Righteousness

Dear Lord, I put on the breastplate of righteousness as a shield from the undue pain the enemy intends for my heart. He knows he can use the pain of loss as a wedge to do me long-term harm. Thank You, Father, for helping me to stand strong against his plan. He wants to keep me hurting, but You would have me healed from my pain. Jesus knew and experienced loss, including the loss of His close friends who betrayed Him. So You know the pain I am feeling. Cover my anger, hurt, and bitterness with Your goodness, mercy, and grace. I need Your grace right now to be the air I breathe and the food I eat. I need You to fill me with Your Spirit as You heal me from this pain. I need Your righteousness because I cannot count on my own. In Christ's name, amen.

Put On the Shoes of Peace

Father, I put on the shoes of peace as I face the torment of grief over what I have lost. Still my rough waters, Lord. Let me walk on the raging seas with the shoes of peace. Speak to me, O Lord, the words "Peace, be still!" [Mark 4:39 NKJV]. Let me experience Your presence as shalom in my heart, God. The storm in my heart feels as wild as a storm on a sea. I speak shalom in my heart, in my mind, and in my emotions. I speak shalom in my feet and in my actions. Let peace prevent me from adding more pain and more loss to this situation by saying or doing something unwise. In Christ's name, amen.

Take Up the Shield of Faith

Lord, with hands weary with grief, I lift up the shield of faith as I overcome the sadness I feel. And Satan, in the name of Christ, I refuse to allow this grief to turn to bitterness. I know your tactics, and they cannot work with me. With the shield of faith, I reject every lie about my loss and my recovery. I have experienced loss before, and I have recovered. I have found new opportunities for laughter and hope when I did not think I could. I will get through this because Christ in me is the hope of glory. In Christ's name, amen.

Take the Helmet of Salvation

Father, I put on the helmet of my salvation as I deal with this terrible loss. I am secure in You, and though I'm rattled by my loss, I take joy in my salvation, which brings calm to the rough patches of life. I take comfort in knowing that even though I have lost something dear to me, I will never lose You, Lord. I will never lose my access to You. You will never leave me or make me feel unworthy of my standing with You. You are eternal and can never die. You are the only One who loves perfectly and never leaves. In the midst of this loss, that security brings me great comfort. In Christ's name, amen.

Take Up the Sword of the Spirit

Lord, the grief associated with this loss is crushing. I know I will get through this, but until I do, I lean hard on You. I pick up the sword of the Spirit—Your Word—and find comfort in my sadness. I use this sword to counter the enemy's attempts to gain a foothold in my life. I know this pain will not last forever because I choose to put my trust in Your goodness and Your presence. Your Word says, "The LORD is near to the brokenhearted and saves the crushed in Spirit" [Psalm 34:18 ESV]. Your Word also tells me that I am blessed in loss and grief because I will find comfort [Matthew 5:4]. I lift up these truths so that the grief and loss that Satan seeks to exacerbate in my life will just make me more blessed and closer to God. Thank You, God, for Your sword of truth. In Christ's name, amen.

Victory

Pray and ask God to reveal any of your thoughts, beliefs, or words that display a spirit of hopelessness and resignation in the face of loss. Consider things you may have said or done that do not reflect trust in God's sovereign hand in the middle of this pain. Write these all down. For each untruth, look for a countering truth from God's Word. When you write down the countering truth, be sure to cross out the untruth and pray, in Christ's name, that it will no longer affect your life and the lives of those around you. Then thank God that the power of His truth has been let loose to do its work of healing, empowerment, and grace in you. Here's an example.

- *Untruth*: I will never be able to let go and get over this.
- *Truth*: "He heals the brokenhearted and binds up their wounds" (Psalm 147:3).

14

PRAYING ABOUT A THORN

*Because of the surpassing greatness of the revelations,
for this reason, to keep me from exalting myself, there
was given me a thorn in the flesh, a messenger of Satan
to torment me—to keep me from exalting myself!*

2 CORINTHIANS 12:7

Thorns come in all shapes and sizes. Some thorns are emotional, such as loneliness, fear, or depression. They could come from painful memories or regrets. Other thorns are relational, such as when someone gets on your nerves or tries to intimidate you. An unhappy marriage can be the most painful of relational thorns. Some thorns are financial or caused by a miserable work situation. Still others might be physical, such as a disability or pain that just doesn't seem to go away. Whatever the thorn, it produces ongoing pain that drives you to your knees to ask God to take it away, just as Paul did.

You can know you are dealing with a thorn when you ask God to take it away—as Paul did—but God chooses not to. Paul had a thorn, and he asked God three times to remove it. But each time, God said no. In fact, God basically said, "You've got this all wrong, Paul. This thorn is actually a gift" (my Evans paraphrase). It was a gift because through this thorn, Paul received the blessing of greater grace and power in his life. "And He [God] has said to me, 'My grace is sufficient for you, for power is perfected in weakness'" (2 Corinthians 12:9). God didn't grant Paul's request, but He did meet his need.

Well, once Paul heard that, he decided he would gladly boast of his weaknesses and thorns because in these, he discovered God's strength and grace. How much grace? Sufficient grace, as we read in verse 9. If you are enduring a thorn—*any* thorn—and God has not removed it, He will give you sufficient grace to bear it and even to become stronger because of it. As Paul wrote, "For when I am weak, then I am strong" (verse 10). If you are dealing with a thorn and God has not removed it, don't try to pull it out. You'll just rip something in the process. Rather, go searching for grace.

Put On the Belt of Truth

Thank You, God, for the grace You give me when I struggle. Thank You for not answering all my prayers the way I want You to. Thank You for the truth of Your Word, which says, "God is able to make all grace abound to you, so that always having all sufficiency in everything, you may have an abundance for every good deed" [2 Corinthians 9:8]. I wear this belt of truth proudly, knowing that in my weakness, Your grace is sufficient for me. In Christ's name, amen.

Put On the Breastplate of Righteousness

Lord, I give You praise and thanksgiving right here in the middle of what You are allowing me to endure. I thank You for blessing me with an extra measure of Your power and grace. You care enough about me to draw me closer to You and make me a better person. You are using this thorn to cultivate in me a greater heart of love than I've ever had.

> We also exult in our tribulations, knowing that tribulation brings about perseverance; and perseverance, proven character; and proven character, hope; and hope does not disappoint, because the love of God has been poured out within our hearts through the Holy Spirit who was given to us [Romans 5:3-5].

Thank You for the hope You are giving me through this trial. In Christ's name, amen.

Put On the Shoes of Peace

Father, I put on the shoes of peace in my heart, mind, and emotions. This thorn that You have allowed to remain has upset me in many ways. It's caused me to worry and become irritated. But in the name of Jesus Christ, I rebuke both worry and irritation and instead choose to carry peace in me. I choose to direct my thoughts toward Your goodness and grace. I ask You to continue to give me an extra measure of grace so that Your peace will flood my spirit. I can't create my own peace, God—not while struggling with this thorn. I need Your grace to be manifest in multiple ways throughout my days to remind me of Your presence and peace. In Christ's name, amen.

Take Up the Shield of Faith

Father God, I don't understand this. I don't get why You are allowing it to continue. I don't like it. It hurts. I've asked You to solve it, fix it, or change it, but You won't. So, Lord, in faith, I choose to praise You in it. I thank You for what You are doing through it. I honor You with words of gratitude and trust, knowing that the shield of faith is a powerful defense against the enemy. So that's why I choose to believe Your promise that in my weakness, I am made strong. In Christ's name, amen.

Take the Helmet of Salvation

Lord, thorns have a way of making me feel unsettled. I'm unsettled about how this situation will turn out or whether it will ever be resolved. That is why I need a great reminder today, God, of the security I find in You. I trust in the salvation that was bought for me on the cross of Christ and the sanctification that is being accomplished in me through the power of the Holy Spirit. Thank You for the grace, God, to know You in this way. In Christ's name, amen.

Take Up the Sword of the Spirit

Heavenly Father, I am blessed. I take up the sword of the Spirit and crush Satan's lies. I know that I am blessed, for Your Word says, "Blessed is the man who remains steadfast under trial, for when he has stood the test he will receive the crown of life, which God has promised to those who love him" [James 1:12 ESV]. I also know I will eventually be restored and strengthened. "After you have suffered a little while, the God of all grace, who has called you to his eternal glory in Christ, will himself restore, confirm, strengthen, and establish you" [1 Peter 5:10 ESV]. And I trust that the glory to be revealed one day will make this thorn seem like a splinter. "For I consider that the sufferings of this present time are not worth comparing with the glory that is to be revealed to us" [Romans 8:18 ESV]. This is the sword that defeats Satan's strategies. In Christ's name, amen.

Victory

Pray and ask God to reveal any of your thoughts, beliefs, or words that weaken your faith that God will use this thorn for your good. Also consider anything you have said to others that reflects a complaining spirit. Write these all down. For each untruth, look for a countering truth from God's Word. When you write down the countering truth, be sure to cross out the untruth and pray, in Christ's name, that it will no longer affect your life and the lives of those around you. Then thank God that the power of His truth has been let loose to do its work of healing, empowerment, and grace in you. Here's an example.

- *Untruth*: I give up.
- *Truth*: "Therefore, do not throw away your confidence, which has a great reward" (Hebrews 10:35).

15

PRAYING FOR MY ENEMIES

You have heard that it was said, "You shall love your neighbor and hate your enemy." But I say to you, love your enemies and pray for those who persecute you, so that you may be sons of your Father who is in heaven.

MATTHEW 5:43-45

This is the part of anyone's prayer list that we always hope is short. No one wants a long list of enemies. But a Christian who is following God will eventually find some enemies. When that happens, the names of those new enemies should quickly become entries on our prayer list.

Stephen, the first Christian we know of who was killed for his faith, prayed one of the most meaningful prayers in the Bible. As the stones were flying toward him, he prayed, "Lord, do not hold this sin against them!" (Acts 7:60).

Who are your enemies? Will you pray for them with the same urgency you pray for your friends?

You can overcome evil with good by praying for God's intervention in the hearts of people who have hurt you. There are two passages that I want you to pray. Every time you read the word "you," I want you to insert the name of the person you are praying for. The first passage is Ephesians 1:16-23, and the second is Colossians 1:9-14.

Do this every day. As you do, keep these verses in mind too:

> This is the confidence which we have before Him, that, if we
> ask anything according to His will, He hears us. And if we
> know that He hears us in whatever we ask, we know that we
> have the requests which we have asked from Him (1 John
> 5:14-15).

> As the rain and the snow come down from heaven,
> And do not return there without watering the earth
> And making it bear and sprout,
> And furnishing seed to the sower and bread to the eater;
> So will My word be which goes forth from My mouth;
> It will not return to Me empty,
> Without accomplishing what I desire,
> And without succeeding in the matter for which I sent it
> (Isaiah 55:10-11).

Pray in confidence that God can change the heart of your enemy.
And if He chooses not to, your heart will be changed through this act of
love for someone who has done you harm. It will soften where it once
was hard, enabling you to freely love and to fully live out your purpose
and God's plan.

Put On the Belt of Truth

Father, Your Word tells me that I will be rewarded if I pray for my enemies and do good to them. Satan wants me to forget this truth, but I
stand in it and ask You to help me to live it out.

> I say to you who hear, love your enemies, do good to those
> who hate you, bless those who curse you, pray for those who
> mistreat you...If you do good to those who do good to you,
> what credit is that to you? For even sinners do the same...But
> love your enemies, and do good, and lend, expecting noth-
> ing in return; and your reward will be great, and you will be

sons of the Most High; for He Himself is kind to ungrateful and evil men [Luke 6:27-28,33,35].

Lord, in my words and actions, may I show kindness toward those who are unkind to me. I know You will reward me. In Christ's name, amen.

Put On the Breastplate of Righteousness

God, I could pray all day, pray through this entire book, and yet if I am harboring bitterness, hate, or anger toward my enemies, You will not hear my prayers. When I do not forgive, my fellowship with You suffers. Your Word tells me to walk in righteousness and to do right by others. "Whenever you stand praying, forgive, if you have anything against anyone, so that your Father who is in heaven will also forgive you your transgressions" [Mark 11:25]. I put on the righteousness of Christ by forgiving my enemies and praying that You will bless them. In Christ's name, amen.

Put On the Shoes of Peace

Lord, sometimes I feel as if I have forgiven my enemies, but then my actions or words reveal that I haven't. Thank You for Your patience as I walk through this process. Continue changing my heart so that I will always desire for You to bless them. Thank You for being patient with me in this process and for reminding me that it is a process. Help me to make steps each day as I learn to trust You completely and let go of the anger and bitterness, the pain and confusion that I sometimes feel. Set me free to fully enjoy the life You have created me to live and the fruitfulness of a close relationship with You. In letting go of my anger, I accept Your peace. In Christ's name, amen.

Take Up the Shield of Faith

With the shield of faith, Lord, I cast down all barriers between me and those who call me an enemy. I choose to bless them rather than curse them. I pray in faith for healing and hope for them. Please do not hold their sins against them, Lord, but forgive them fully. I have faith that You will show all of us the error of our ways. I pray that we can all grow to become more Christlike each and every day. In Christ's name, amen.

Take the Helmet of Salvation

God, today the helmet of salvation is mine. I take it with joy and pray salvation for my enemies. I pray they will seek You with all their heart and join me in wearing this great helmet, which represents Your saving power. If any of my enemies do not know You as Lord and Savior, I pray that You will bring people into their lives who will introduce them to You. I pray that You will make their hearts receptive to Your Word and Your salvation. And for those who do know You, I pray for Your sanctifying grace and mercy to draw them closer to You than ever before. In Christ's name, amen.

Take Up the Sword of the Spirit

Father, I know the enemy of my soul is the great separator, the great divider of people. I know he hates unity and harmony. Today, I take up the sword of the Spirit and pray against his divisive tactics in the name of Jesus Christ. I rebuke all satanic influences at work in my enemies' lives and in my own life. I pray for deep conviction of sin and the gentle wooing of Your Holy Spirit in all of us that we may be one, as You desire us to be one [John 17:21].

Victory

Pray and ask God to reveal your unkind thoughts, beliefs, or words about your enemies. Also consider anything that they have said about you that is unkind and untrue. In addition, look for any resistance on your part to be reconciled in Christ with your enemies. Write these all down. For each untruth, look for a countering truth from God's Word. When you write down the countering truth, be sure to cross out the untruth and pray, in Christ's name, that it will no longer affect your life and the lives of those around you. Then thank God that the power of His truth has been let loose to do its work of healing, empowerment, and grace in you. Here's an example.

- *Untruth*: I never want to see that person again.

- *Truth*: "If you see the donkey of one who hates you lying down under its burden, you shall refrain from leaving him with it; you shall rescue it with him" (Exodus 23:5 ESV).

16

OVERCOMING PAST FAILURES

Who is the one who condemns? Christ Jesus is He
who died, yes, rather who was raised, who is at the
right hand of God, who also intercedes for us.

ROMANS 8:34

One of the greatest things about God's grace is His ability to turn a mess into a miracle. I'm not saying that God endorses failures or that He accepts sin. He doesn't. But God can take our failures and use them for good. Consider Peter, to whom Jesus said, "Simon, Simon, behold, Satan has demanded permission to sift you like wheat; but I have prayed for you, that your faith may not fail; and you, when once you have turned again, strengthen your brothers" (Luke 22:31-32).

In that statement, Jesus Christ foretold Peter's failure. Yet even though the words came from Christ Himself, Peter still thought he had everything under control. "But he said to Him, 'Lord, with You I am ready to go both to prison and to death!'" (verse 33).

Peter didn't accept the prediction. He didn't own up to his own frailty. But Jesus was right, and Peter failed. Peter created a mess, and God allowed it in order to better equip him for ministry. Jesus had hinted of this process: "Once you have turned again, strengthen your brothers." Some of our messes, mistakes, and sins come about simply because of our own flaws or rebellion. God allows other failures to happen because

He knows that when you come back, you will be better prepared for ministry—your perspective will be purer, and your commitment will be stronger. At times God allows Satan to trip you up in order to teach you something about yourself and about Him.

So when we repent, God turns the bad into something useful. That doesn't excuse our bad behavior or remove its consequences. It just means that God is bigger than our failure.

God didn't turn His back on Peter because of his sin. In fact, He did just the opposite—God pursued him. He made sure Peter knew He still cared. The angel at the empty tomb specifically said, "But go, tell His disciples *and Peter*..." (Mark 16:7). Don't forget Peter, the angel said. I know he's blown it. I know he's dropped the ball. And that's why I'm singling out his name—God wants him to know He still cares.

Despite your failures and sins, God calls your name too. Listen, and you will hear Him. He still has a blessing to give you and a purpose for you to fulfill.

Put On the Belt of Truth

Lord, I know everyone fails at something. Still, my failures seem so large to me, and the regret I feel is so hard to overcome. But the truth is, failures can become victories in the long run. Eve failed. Adam failed. Abraham failed. Moses failed. Jacob failed. David failed. Peter failed. Down through history, many Christians have experienced great failures. Lord, You were able to turn things around and bring about a great purpose for them in the end. I claim that truth—that promise—for my own life. Bring good out of my greatest failures and use them to shape my heart and character in a way that reflects You all the more. In Christ's name, amen.

Put On the Breastplate of Righteousness

Father, with the breastplate of righteousness firmly in place, I choose to believe You can free me from my failures. My failures taunt me and make me feel unrighteous and unworthy. However, I stand on Your promise for forgiveness for all my unrighteousness. Satan, you have no ground for continuing to point out my unrighteous acts or words. Every one of them is forgiven. "Therefore there is now no condemnation for those who are in Christ Jesus" [Romans 8:1]. In Christ's name, amen.

Put On the Shoes of Peace

I praise You, Lord, for the shoes of peace, which help me to walk away from my every failure. Not only that, I can also walk toward restoration and success in the days ahead. By walking in the shoes of peace, I walk in Your footsteps, Lord. As I put on the shoes of peace every day, may I also enjoy thoughts of peace regarding myself. In Christ's name, amen.

Take Up the Shield of Faith

Father, everyone who overcame failure in the Bible overcame by faith. They were all imperfect, and many of them had failed miserably. I, too, have received faith to stand against the taunts of the enemy, and I choose to take up that faith right now regarding my past. I will learn from my past, but I will not live in it. In faith, I lift up this promise from Your Word:

> Do not call to mind the former things,
> Or ponder things of the past.
> Behold, I will do something new,
> Now it will spring forth;
> Will you not be aware of it?
> I will even make a roadway in the wilderness,
> Rivers in the desert [Isaiah 43:18-19].

I take up the shield of faith and ward off condemning words of the enemy that tell me my past will determine my future. I am not bound by my past failures because I trust You are doing something new. Satan, in Jesus's name, I refuse your constant reminders of how I have failed.

God knows my past and has prepared a forgiven and victorious future for me. In Christ's name, amen.

Take the Helmet of Salvation

Lord, Your helmet of salvation protects me from the continuing accusations of the enemy about my past failures. I am a new creation. I am not of the old Adam, who must follow the ways of the flesh. I am new, born of the Spirit, and I can overcome any past failure. Thank You for this valuable truth. Satan, in the name of Jesus Christ who defeated you at the cross, I withstand all the reminders and accusations you hurl at me about my past failures. They are covered by the blood of Christ and have no more power over me. In Christ's name I pray these things, amen.

Take Up the Sword of the Spirit

Lord, Your Word, the sword of the Spirit, is a book full of victories. Many men and women in the Bible suffered great failure, but their lives and futures all changed forever when they trusted in You. Satan, I take up the sword, which is truth, to silence your vain reminders of something God has chosen to forget. It is written, "I, even I, am the one who wipes out your transgressions for My own sake, and I will not remember your sins" [Isaiah 43:25]. In Christ's name, amen.

Victory

Pray and ask God to reveal your thoughts, beliefs, or words about your past failures that are rooted in regret, shame, or hopelessness. Also consider anything others may have said to you about things you have done wrong. Write these all down. For each untruth, look for a countering truth from God's Word. When you write down the countering truth, be sure to cross out the untruth and pray, in Christ's name, that it will no longer affect your life and the lives of those around you. Then thank God that the power of His truth has been let loose to do its work of healing, empowerment, and grace in you. Here's an example.

- *Untruth*: God would never use someone with a past like mine.

- *Truth*: "Praise the LORD, my soul; all my inmost being, praise his holy name. Praise the LORD, my soul, and forget not all his benefits—who forgives all your sins and heals all your diseases, who redeems your life from the pit and crowns you with love and compassion, who satisfies your desires with good things so that your youth is renewed like the eagle's" (Psalm 103:1-5 NIV).

17

PRAYING FOR MY MATE

Husbands ought also to love their own wives as their own bodies.
He who loves his own wife loves himself.

EPHESIANS 5:28

Wives, be subject to your own husbands, as to the Lord.

EPHESIANS 5:22

Intercession is prayer on behalf of another. In marriage, we're called to intercede for our mate. Sometimes when we're not happy with a certain habit or attitude in our spouse, we complain about it. But there's a better way—why not pray for your life partner? Here are some specific things to pray he/she will enjoy:

- a rich spiritual life and intimate relationship with the Lord
- health
- God's guidance
- wisdom
- a deeper love relationship with you

There are no doubt other topics that specifically apply to your mate. You may need to ask God to show you how to pray for your mate. The important thing is that you *do* pray—regularly and throughout each day.

When you feel like complaining, choose instead to take your concern to God. When you feel like questioning, go to God and ask Him to clarify the issue for you. When you feel as if your spouse needs to improve in an area, tell God specifically what it is.

Sometimes you will discover that when you pray for your mate, God will actually do a work in you. He will either help you to see things differently or show you an area where you need to grow. Be open to God's answers to your prayers—they may be different from what you expect, but they will always improve your marriage.

If you are not married, you can pray these prayers for your future spouse or for a couple who could use your help fighting on their behalf in the war room.

Put On the Belt of Truth

Lord, thank You for my spouse. Though we sometimes argue and don't always see eye to eye, I know You brought us together. Forgive me for questioning this at times. Your truth stands—"What therefore God has joined together, let no man separate" [Mark 10:9]. "No man" includes me, Lord. Help me not to divide us emotionally or spiritually, Lord, by fighting with my mate rather than fighting my battles in my war room. In Christ's name, amen.

Put On the Breastplate of Righteousness

Father, You are my righteousness. May my mate see in me the effects of righteousness as I live as a testimony to Your love. I pray that You will make me a model of peace, kindness, gentleness, and love to my spouse. May I embody a spirit of grace and patience, Lord. I want to live righteously in my marriage, Lord, because righteousness is a weapon against the enemy. So stop me in my tracks before my thoughts or actions lead me down any wrong path. And do the same for my spouse. In Christ's name, amen.

Put On the Shoes of Peace

Dear heavenly Father, I pray for peace for my spouse and for our marriage. Peace of mind, peace emotionally, and peace in our relationship with each other. May we each put on the comfortable shoes of peace that enable us to stand firm as a couple under the banner of Your peace. When we start to argue and it becomes heated, remind us of Your peace. Calm our hearts and our minds, Lord, so that we do not give Satan victory in this area of our lives. In Christ's name, amen.

Take Up the Shield of Faith

Lord, You have said that even mustard-sized faith can move a mountain. I pray that when my mate and I face mountains that threaten our unity, You'll honor our faith, no matter how small, and use it to bring about great results. Praying to You right now is an act of faith, so I pray in faith that You will bring my spouse's heart and mind in line under Yours. I know that whatever I ask according to Your will, You hear me and will give me what I ask, so I thank You for this ahead of time [1 John 5:14-15]. In faith, I thank You for removing every obstacle that blocks our way to fully maximizing the purpose You have brought us together to fulfill. Lord, I believe You will do this. Where necessary, please help my unbelief [Mark 9:24].

Take the Helmet of Salvation

Father, You have saved us for Yourself. You have given us new life by Your Spirit so that we will no longer follow the desires of our flesh. I trust in Your salvation to keep me and my mate in unity to the end of our days. I put on the helmet of salvation, which guards my mind from jealousy, anger, and bitterness. I reject the enemy's whispered thoughts and accusations against my mate, and I fully accept my spouse as he/she is, knowing that neither of us is perfect and never will be. Help me to continually align my thoughts with Yours. Grant me a love like Yours, which is forever secure no matter what either my spouse or I do. For You have said,

"I will betroth you to me forever. I will betroth you to me in righteousness and in justice, in steadfast love and in mercy" [Hosea 2:19 ESV]. In Christ's name, amen.

Take Up the Sword of the Spirit
Lord, Your Word teaches us about love:

- Love is patient and kind; love does not envy or boast; it is not arrogant or rude. It does not insist on its own way; it is not irritable or resentful; it does not rejoice at wrongdoing, but rejoices with the truth. Love bears all things, believes all things, hopes all things, endures all things [1 Corinthians 13:4-7 ESV].

- He who finds a wife finds a good thing and obtains favor from the LORD [Proverbs 18:22 ESV].

- Let each one of you love his wife as himself, and let the wife see that she respects her husband [Ephesians 5:33 ESV].

- You husbands in the same way, live with your wives in an understanding way, as with someone weaker, since she is a woman; and show her honor as a fellow heir of the grace of life, so that your prayers will not be hindered [1 Peter 3:7].

Lord, I embrace these truths today. In Christ's name, amen.

Victory

Pray and ask God to reveal any negative thoughts, beliefs, or words concerning your spouse. Also consider anything your spouse may have said or done to you that does not reflect God's truth or His love. Write these all down. For each untruth, look for a countering truth from God's Word. When you write down the countering truth, be sure to cross out the untruth and pray, in Christ's name, that it will no longer affect your life and the lives of those around you. Then thank God that the power of His truth has been let loose to do its work of healing, empowerment, and grace in you. Here's an example.

- *Untruth*: I can change my spouse by telling him/her what to do.
- *Truth*: "If I speak with the tongues of men and of angels, but do not have love, I have become a noisy gong or a clanging cymbal" (1 Corinthians 13:1).

18

OVERCOMING ADDICTIONS

Do not get drunk with wine, for that is dissipation,
but be filled with the Spirit.

EPHESIANS 5:18

Most substance addictions don't come on a person suddenly. Rather, they develop as the person first experiments and then continues using the substance until there is a physical and psychological dependence. That's when the addicted person craves the substance to which he or she is addicted. This can be a difficult stronghold, but the power of God to break addictions is stronger yet.

A chemical stronghold is a dependency on chemicals to address, escape, cope with, or find relief from the struggles and stresses of life. People with chemical strongholds often reveal themselves easily. They may say, "I just need a drink to unwind," or "I just need a smoke to reduce the stress," or even "I'm ugly until I get my first cup of coffee." All three have said the same thing: I cannot be what I was meant to be without ingesting these chemicals. Sure, coffee is not similar to cocaine in terms of its effects, but it stems from the same root—looking to chemicals to address a spiritual need.

The problem comes from using something in the physical world to fix a spiritual pain, lack, or emptiness. It would be like a guy wrapping Band-Aids around his chest because his girlfriend broke his heart.

Or someone who drank a lot of milk because she desired to grow spiritually. Neither would do any good at all. A spiritual problem must be addressed spiritually.

Our bodies are temples of the living God, and anything that controls us makes us slaves to something other than God.

> Therefore do not let sin reign in your mortal body so that you obey its lusts, and do not go on presenting the members of your body to sin as instruments of unrighteousness; but present yourselves to God as those alive from the dead, and your members as instruments of righteousness to God. For sin shall not be master over you, for you are not under law but under grace (Romans 6:12-14).

That drink, cigarette, pill, cup of coffee, drug—whatever you are struggling with—is not to be your master. Because of God's grace, you have been made alive in Him, and you are now free to choose your responses—if you will align yourself with the truth of God's solution to your stronghold. Every time you choose a chemical substance, God gives you a moment to choose Him instead. Seize that moment each and every time, asking Him to meet You right there and to divert your craving away from something that would enslave you and toward Him who sets you free.

Put On the Belt of Truth

Father God, I put on Your belt of truth as I stand against the addictions that would destroy me. The truth is that through Christ, I can resist the magnetic pull of the substances that have lured me. I am dead to the sin of addiction and fully alive to God through the resurrection power of Jesus Christ. Lord, may the truth of my identity in You protect me when I am tempted to return to my addiction. While I still have ears to hear, remind me to turn to You. And place people in my life who will walk with me through this to victory. In Christ's name, amen.

Put On the Breastplate of Righteousness

Lord, my righteous state through the blood of Christ is my breastplate, protecting me from the enemy's poison-tainted arrows. With this armor, I stand strong in the battle for my soul. Your righteousness prevails against all the attempts of the enemy to lure me back into my unrighteous addictions. When I wear the breastplate of righteousness, there is no place for addictions in my life. Thank You for not leaving me alone in this. Thank You for victory in Your name—I have overcome because You have overcome. In Christ's name, amen.

Put On the Shoes of Peace

God, I know many of my temptations to addictive substances are attempts to self-medicate my wounds and find peace and calm. But with the shoes of peace that You provide in Christ, I need no other medication for my soul. Your peace is enough to guard my soul in the roughest battle. I seek Your peace right now, God. I need Your peace. I choose Your peace, Lord, and I thank You for its power to soothe my heart, ease my mind, and calm my fears. In Christ's name, amen.

Take Up the Shield of Faith

From time to time, Lord, I see the enemy's arrows of temptation flying toward me. At such times, I take up the shield of faith against those fiery darts. I repel every advance of my adversary with this mighty shield. Lord, I hold it up high and watch the enemy retreat as his missiles fall harmlessly to the ground. My faith is in You, Lord, knowing You have not left me, despite how low I have sunk. You have forgiven me for the things I have done while under the influence of substances. You can restore that which has caused me pain to begin with. I have faith that no challenge is too difficult for You to win. In Christ's name, amen.

Take the Helmet of Salvation

Thank You, Father, for Your salvation, which is a helmet against the destructive thoughts of my enemy. Thank You for a helmet of salvation that prevents the desires of my addiction from taking hold of my mind, demanding satisfaction. I praise You, Father, for this strong defense against the enemy. I put it on right now and remind myself of my security, strength, and power in You. I am a new creation in You, and so I can overcome these chemical strongholds. In Christ's name, amen.

Take Up the Sword of the Spirit

God, I take up the sword of the Spirit against Satan's lies, and I stand in this truth:

> No temptation has overtaken you that is not common to man. God is faithful, and he will not let you be tempted beyond your ability, but with the temptation he will also provide the way of escape, that you may be able to endure it [1 Corinthians 10:13 ESV].

I also choose to be sober-minded and watchful, knowing that Satan is looking for a way to devour me [1 Peter 5:8]. Father, I proclaim this truth over my life: "Submit yourselves therefore to God. Resist the devil and he will flee from you" [James 4:7]. In Christ's name, amen.

Victory

Pray and ask God to bring to mind any of your thoughts, beliefs, or words that reveal a mindset of defeat related to any addiction—to chemicals, overspending, gossip, entertainment, sex...Consider things others may have said to you that reinforce the idea that these addictions are okay or unbeatable. Write these all down. For each untruth, look for a countering truth from God's Word. When you write down the countering truth, be sure to cross out the untruth and pray, in Christ's name, that it will no longer affect your life and the lives of those around you. Then thank God that the power of His truth has been let loose to do its work of healing, empowerment, and grace in you. Here's an example.

- *Untruth*: Don't be legalistic. It's okay to drink.

- *Truth*: "'All things are lawful for me,' but not all things are helpful. 'All things are lawful for me,' but I will not be dominated by anything" (1 Corinthians 6:12 ESV).

19

BREAKING FREE FROM FINANCIAL BONDAGE

Owe nothing to anyone except to love one another;
for he who loves his neighbor has fulfilled the law.

ROMANS 13:8

Scripture tells us that living in debt is abnormal for a Christian. We read in Psalm 37:21, "The wicked borrows and does not pay back, but the righteous is gracious and gives." In fact, God makes a direct connection between financial accountability and spiritual responsibility.

> He who is faithful in a very little thing is faithful also in much; and he who is unrighteous in a very little thing is unrighteous also in much. Therefore if you have not been faithful in the use of unrighteous wealth, who will entrust the true riches to you? (Luke 16:10-11).

The Bible does not condemn legitimate borrowing, but it does condemn borrowing in such a way that you're not able to pay it back—or pay it back without incurring a substantial loss.

A refusal to handle money God's way can actually limit God's responsiveness to your requests for greater things. If you are a parent, you understand this firsthand. Say you gave your child $5 to spend or to save, but your child lost it or squandered it on arcade games. Would you be so quick as to give your child another $5? Or would you want to teach your child some important money principles first and then watch to be sure your child was applying these principles in life?

God's solution to financial bondage can be summarized with three simple words: give, save, and spend—in that order. Your financial freedom is inextricably tied to that system.

Put On the Belt of Truth

Lord, You've been good to me. You have provided for my needs, and everything I have can be traced back to Your hand of provision. Help me be a good steward of my blessings. Remind me to always obey Your truth about managing my money. I put on the belt of truth rather than the money belt of greed. I do this by putting You first in all things because I can serve only one Master [Matthew 6:24]. In Christ's name, amen.

Put On the Breastplate of Righteousness

Father, as I handle the money You've entrusted to me, may I do so wearing the breastplate of righteousness and dealing righteously in all my financial transactions. Give me wisdom as I spend so I can make right choices with the money You have given to me. Help me to help others. Guide me in ways that allow my resources to extend and advance Your kingdom. Show me how to honor You with the money You have given to me. As I make right choices, You will deliver me from debt and financial bondage. I pray in Jesus's name against a spirit of greed and dependence on money. In Christ's name, amen.

Put On the Shoes of Peace

Lord, with the shoes of peace, I need not be anxious about money matters but can rest peacefully, knowing that You're aware of my every need. There is no need for me to be anxious or worry about money. You give me true peace, and whenever I need provision, You see to it abundantly. In Christ's name, amen.

Take Up the Shield of Faith

Dear Father, the enemy comes at me with accusations and thoughts that You won't provide for my needs. The enemy also makes me feel that some of my wants are actually needs. Or that it's my fault that I am in the financial situation I'm in because of overspending or greed. I have faith that when I repent, You forgive me. You deliver me when I put Your truth into practice and seek to honor You with my resources. I have faith that when I give to others—whether my money, my time, or anything else—it will also be given to me [Luke 6:38]. When things are tight and yet I still give, Lord, let that be an action of faith. In Christ's name, amen.

Take the Helmet of Salvation

Lord, You bought me at a price when You saved me through the death, burial, and resurrection of Jesus Christ. My salvation came at no small cost to You. Because of this I especially want to honor You in all that You have given me. It's Yours anyhow. Because of Christ's new creation in me, I will use my resources for Your glory. Deliver me from financial bondage, Lord, and make me a giver who honors You completely. In Christ's name, amen.

Take Up the Sword of the Spirit

God, I will follow Your command to stop worrying about money.

> For this reason I say to you, do not be worried about your life, as to what you will eat or what you will drink; nor for your body, as to what you will put on. Is not life more than food, and the body more than clothing? Look at the birds of the air, that they do not sow, nor reap nor gather into barns, and yet your heavenly Father feeds them. Are you not worth much more than they? And who of you by being worried can add a single hour to his life? And why are you worried about clothing? Observe how the lilies of the field grow; they do not toil nor do they spin, yet I say to you that

not even Solomon in all his glory clothed himself like one of these. But if God so clothes the grass of the field, which is alive today and tomorrow is thrown into the furnace, will He not much more clothe you? You of little faith! Do not worry then, saying, "What will we eat?" or "What will we drink?" or "What will we wear for clothing?" For the Gentiles eagerly seek all these things; for your heavenly Father knows that you need all these things. But seek first His kingdom and His righteousness, and all these things will be added to you [Matthew 6:25-33].

In Christ's name, amen.

Victory

Pray and ask God to remind you of any of your thoughts, beliefs, or words that reveal a heart of greed. Also consider any of your purchases or actions that did not honor God with your money. Write these all down. For each untruth, look for a countering truth from God's Word. When you write down the countering truth, be sure to cross out the untruth and pray, in Christ's name, that it will no longer affect your life and the lives of those around you. Then thank God that the power of His truth has been let loose to do its work of healing, empowerment, and grace in you. Here's an example.

- *Untruth*: I won't be able to make ends meet.
- *Truth*: "My God will supply all your needs according to His riches in glory in Christ Jesus" (Philippians 4:19).

20

GETTING PAST FOOD STRONGHOLDS

Whether, then, you eat or drink or whatever you do,
do all to the glory of God.

1 CORINTHIANS 10:31

One of the most overlooked strongholds in America today is that of eating. Often it isn't even viewed as a stronghold. In fact, in Christian circles, we will frequently condemn the alcoholic, the drug addict, or the porn addict, all the while excusing the food addict. But food strongholds dominate a large percentage of the population and contribute to most of our health problems. An eating stronghold doesn't always show up through a person eating too much food. Eating strongholds also show up in people who won't eat enough food (anorexia) or people who eat too much food but then purge (bulimia).

Paul directs us to an Old Testament example of how God views misplaced desire. We read first about this example in the book of Psalms, where it talks about the Israelites complaining against God in the wilderness after they had been set free from the Egyptians (Psalm 78:19-21,25,27-31). Paul elaborates on this situation.

With most of them God was not well-pleased...

Now these things happened as examples for us, so that we would not crave evil things as they also craved. Do not be idolaters, as some of them were; as it is written, "The people sat down to eat and drink, and stood up to play" (1 Corinthians 10:5-7).

In verse 31, God tells us that we are not to place our desires for food above our desire for Him. Rather, food must be brought into its proper perspective underneath the purposes and program of God. Your god, or your idol, is whatever you obey. If food calls to you and you obey it outside of God's will for its use in your body, you have made food an idol.

The solution to overcoming an eating stronghold in your life can be found in grace. Remember, grace is what God does for you. A diet is what you do for yourself. Cutting back on this or eating more of that is law. It can last a minute, but it rarely lasts long because law does not lead to life. The principle of grace reminds you that you are uniquely created to bring glory to God through your life and with your body (1 Corinthians 6:20).

Just as you wouldn't walk into a beautiful, expensive public building and spray graffiti all over the walls, you won't desecrate your body when you remember who you really are. God says you have been purchased at a very high price—the blood of His Son Jesus Christ. You are not a closeout special or an item on the clearance rack. God paid top dollar for you, and He wants you to treat your body in a way that reflects that value. When you view and value your body as a tool for reflecting God's glory, you're not likely to surrender it to anything that might bring it harm.

Put On the Belt of Truth

Lord, I stand in the truth that I can do all things through Him who strengthens me, including eating only until I'm full or eating what I need to instead of avoiding food. Food does not have control over me. If I need to stop eating something, I can stop eating it in Christ's strength. If I need to eat better foods, I can eat them through Christ's strength in me. I have died with Christ to the desires of this world, so I will no longer be controlled by them, but by the Spirit of God. In Christ's name, amen.

Put On the Breastplate of Righteousness

Father, I am to love You with all my heart and with all my soul and with all my might [Deuteronomy 6:5]. Your divine power has granted me everything I need to live a full life through knowing You, who called me by Your own glory and excellence [2 Peter 1:3]. I have been raised up with Christ and am to seek the things above, where Christ is, seated at Your right hand [Colossians 3:1]. When I live in the righteousness of these truths, God, food has no say over me. I have a say over food. In Christ's name, amen.

Put On the Shoes of Peace

Father in heaven, because of Your goodness, You instructed the Israelites to observe a holy day by celebrating: "Eat of the fat, drink of the sweet, and send portions to him who has nothing prepared, for this day is holy to our Lord. Do not be grieved, for the joy of the LORD is your strength" (Nehemiah 8:10). I ask for that joy to show up in my life at this moment and for it to be an ever-present part of my life. Help me to recognize Your joy in my life and to turn to it to find deep satisfaction. And while I am enjoying and celebrating Your goodness and all that You have supplied, guard me with Your peace in Christ so that I do not indulge in excess. In Christ's name, amen.

Take Up the Shield of Faith

Dear Father, I lift up my shield of faith, "for whatever is born of God overcomes the world; and this is the victory that has overcome the world—our faith" [1 John 5:4]. I also stand in faith that I am an overcomer. "Who is the one who overcomes the world, but he who believes that Jesus is the Son of God?" [verse 5]. Father in heaven, I have overcome the world because I am born of You. This victory is mine, so please show me how to walk in it. When I look at food that I should not be eating, remind me that my faith in You has given me all that I need to overcome the temptation in front of me. Satisfy me with the truth that my belief in Jesus Christ, Your Son, is enough to overcome the world. In Christ's name, amen.

Take the Helmet of Salvation

"The grace of God has appeared, bringing salvation to all men, instructing us to deny ungodliness and worldly desires and to live sensibly, righteously and godly in the present age" [Titus 2:11-12]. So Satan, I resist you in the name of Jesus and by the grace of God. I am looking for the blessed hope and the appearing of the glory of our great God and Savior, Christ Jesus [verse 13]. I have more than enough with which to be content.

Take Up the Sword of the Spirit

"Everything created by God is good, and nothing is to be rejected if it is received with gratitude, for it is sanctified by means of the word of God and prayer" [1 Timothy 4:4-5]. I receive the food that You give with gratitude, Lord. Help me to use food in a way that pleases and honors You. Sanctify this food for Your purposes. And thank You for satisfying me with the life of Christ in me. I look to Him to meet the hunger not only in my body but also in my soul.

Victory

Pray and ask God to reveal any thoughts, beliefs, or words indicating that you are placing food in a position higher than God. Is your desire for food too strong to resist? Are you using your eating habits to feel as if you are in control? Consider the times when you have turned to comfort food instead going to the God of all comfort first. Write these all down. For each untruth, look for a countering truth from God's Word. When you write down the countering truth, be sure to cross out the untruth and pray, in Christ's name, that it will no longer affect your life and the lives of those around you. Then thank God that the power of His truth has been let loose to do its work of healing, empowerment, and grace in you. Here's an example.

- *Untruth*: This hurts too much.
- *Truth*: "Blessed be the God and Father of our Lord Jesus Christ, the Father of mercies and God of all comfort, who comforts us in all our affliction" (2 Corinthians 1:3-4).

21

OVERCOMING BITTERNESS

Let all bitterness and wrath and anger and clamor and
slander be put away from you, along with all malice.

EPHESIANS 4:31

Bitterness is a root that can choke out our spiritual life. It often develops small—something unkind was said to us or even just hinted at. Or maybe it was a real or perceived offense. Regardless of what caused it, that small root of bitterness can lodge in our hearts and become a stronghold. When the root first appears, deal with it immediately. Don't wait until it's become a thorn in your heart. Satan loves to use bitterness as an inroad to lead you into sin. Scripture warns us, "See to it that no one comes short of the grace of God; that no root of bitterness springing up causes trouble, and by it many be defiled" (Hebrews 12:15).

Bitterness gives the devil a foothold in your life, and that can lead to a cycle of sin that keeps you from fully living out your destiny. Satan would like nothing more than to keep you from fulfilling the plan God has for you to advance God's kingdom on earth. This is why we are told, "'In your anger do not sin': Do not let the sun go down while you are still angry, and do not give the devil a foothold" (Ephesians 4:26-27 NIV).

We begin overcoming bitterness by trusting that God is sovereign.

If you own a dog, you probably own a leash. The leash grants your dog a degree of freedom, depending on how long the leash is, so he can move about. Yet there comes a point when your dog goes too far, based on the length you have allowed. When he reaches this point, the leash produces resistance, keeping your dog within the boundaries you have set. You are controlling the distance.

I know it may not always seem like it, but the people who have hurt you are on a leash. Even Satan is on a leash—our sovereign God controls how far the devil can go and what he can do. We find a great biblical example of this in the life of Job. When Satan asked for permission to send Job through a trial, God set the boundaries of how far the devil could go.

Joseph provides another example. The greatest statement in history on this principle reveals a powerful truth that will help you overcome bitterness. It's Joseph's reply to his brothers, who had betrayed him. He said, "As for you, you meant evil against me, but God meant it for good in order to bring about this present result, to preserve many people alive" (Genesis 50:20).

Joseph's brothers intended evil against Joseph, but God used that same evil for good. In God's sovereignty, He uses everything—the good and the bad—to take you where you need to go.

Put On the Belt of Truth

Lord, I know bitterness takes root when I believe lies instead of the truth. It also takes root when I choose to view the truth of what happened to me without the lens of Your sovereignty. You allowed it, for whatever reason. Help me as I guard against the root of bitterness by living according to this truth and by closing my ears when the enemy tempts me to question Your goodness and control. In Christ's name, amen.

Put On the Breastplate of Righteousness

Father, the bitterness creeping into my heart hurts me. It's like a weapon that's hijacking my spiritual well-being. For that reason, I put on the breastplate of righteousness to guard my heart from the wounds of bitterness. Help me as I remove this present pain, and keep me on the lookout for future seeds of bitterness so I can deal with them right away and not let them take root. Thank You, Lord, that even if what was done to me was intended for evil, You are a righteous God who will use it for good when I trust in You. Thank You for Your protective breastplate of righteousness when I follow Your Word, which says, "Know this, my beloved brothers: let every person be quick to hear, slow to speak, slow to anger; for the anger of man does not produce the righteousness of God" [James 1:19-20 ESV]. In Christ's name, amen.

Put On the Shoes of Peace

God, the shoes of peace on my feet teach me to forgive real or perceived offenses. I simply cannot walk in peace and hold a grudge. When wearing these shoes, I'm reminded of whom I need to forgive and whom I need to ask to forgive me. Thank You, Father, for these shoes of peace. They lead me to the healing waters. In Christ's name, amen.

Take Up the Shield of Faith

Lord, I know Satan is the accuser of the brethren [Revelation 12:10]. Sometimes when he accuses others of wrongs, I listen to him, agree with him, and harbor a grudge. But I lift up the shield of faith, trusting that You have a purpose for this pain. I cast down those darts of accusation and choose to remain at peace with all others. I will forgive every offense because You have forgiven every offense of mine. I have faith that You will use this for good, Lord. I know You will. Freely I have been forgiven, so freely I forgive others. In Christ's name, amen.

Take the Helmet of Salvation

Father, with the helmet of salvation, I reject the lies of the enemy that accuse others of offenses or remind me of my offenses that You have already forgiven. Thank You, Lord, that the helmet protects me from accusations—Satan's small seeds that take root and grow into lifelong grudges. Though I have sinned against You, You have made me secure in Your love. I want to help others feel secure in my love for them. I choose to forgive and let go of bitterness. In Christ's name, amen.

Take Up the Sword of the Spirit

Dear Lord, the sword of the Spirit makes short work of the enemy's lies and reminders. I will not let these seeds of bitterness sprout in my heart. Rather, I use the sword to cut them off at the root by declaring, in Christ's name, that I will put away "all bitterness and wrath and anger and clamor and slander...along with all malice" [Ephesians 4:31 ESV]. I know that "hatred stirs up strife, but love covers all offenses" [Proverbs 10:12 ESV]. I choose love. The Word declares me forgiven, and therefore I declare all others forgiven of any offenses against me. In Christ's name, amen.

Victory

Pray and ask God to reveal any of your thoughts, beliefs, or words that reflect a spirit of bitterness. Write these all down. For each untruth, look for a countering truth from God's Word. When you write down the countering truth, be sure to cross out the untruth and pray, in Christ's name, that it will no longer affect your life and the lives of those around you. Then thank God that the power of His truth has been let loose to do its work of healing, empowerment, and grace in you. Here's an example.

- *Untruth*: That person is one of the dumbest, most selfish people I know.

- *Truth*: "If anyone thinks he is religious and does not bridle his tongue but deceives his heart, this person's religion is worthless" (James 1:26 ESV).

22

RECEIVING HEALING FROM SICKNESS

*Beloved, I pray that in all respects you may prosper
and be in good health, just as your soul prospers.*

3 John 2

Ill health can be a result of several different causes. If we don't eat right or exercise, our bodies' immune system will be weakened, and we'll be more susceptible to sickness. Some illnesses come from being around someone with a contagious disease. Some can result from a genetic predisposition to that illness. Some, however, can be a result of Satan's direct attack on our bodies.

Whatever the cause of sickness, it's never wrong to pray for healing. The Old and New Testaments include many instances of healing as a result of prayer. When the illness is of satanic origin, warfare is called for. We turn to God for His healing power, and we come down hard against the demonic nature of the illness. And we always cooperate with our bodies' need for restoration by treating them properly as we continue to pray for healing.

You may not be sick at this time, but you probably know someone who is sick. Or you can use these prayers as protection against sicknesses that Satan would like to see inflicted on you. Feel free to use them for yourself or on behalf of someone else. I know that when I've been sick, the prayers of those around me have brought me peace and contributed to my healing. I have also prayed for loved ones in their hour of need. We can help each other heal by doing battle in the heavenlies.

Put On the Belt of Truth

Praise You, Lord, for being our Healer. No matter how bad the situation may look, You still are in control. You continue to hear our prayers and answer them. So, Lord, I summon my measure of faith and the truth of Your Word, asking You to bring my body into good health, which You provide in the atonement. Grant me healing from this present affliction, and bring wholeness and health to my body once again. In Christ's name, amen.

Put On the Breastplate of Righteousness

Lord, righteousness is health of spirit. I thank You for the breastplate of righteousness and ask that it guard me from sickness of body. Allow me, O God, to walk in good health and prosper bodily, even as my soul prospers [3 John 2]. I also ask for Your forgiveness for any way I have contributed to the stress or dis-ease in my body. Help me to make better food choices, Lord, and also to get the adequate rest and exercise my body needs. In addition, give me a righteous mind that is set on You, Lord, because worry, anxiety, and depression can contribute to sickness. In Christ's name, amen.

Put On the Shoes of Peace

Father, today I put on the shoes of peace, which bring healing to my body and soul. I pray for a trusting spirit as I do spiritual battle over this present illness. With these shoes, may my peaceful walk be toward restored health. Lord, I speak peace into the cells of my body. I speak peace into my thoughts. I speak peace into the organs and hormones that my body needs to function well. I thank You for Your peace, which can calm the waves and cure my body. In Christ's name, amen.

Take Up the Shield of Faith

Lord, Jesus sometimes said to those who begged for healing, "Your faith has made you well" [Mark 5:34; 10:52; Luke 8:48; 17:19]. And You healed a boy when his father cried out, "I do believe; help my unbelief" [Mark 9:24]. So I cry out from behind the shield of faith, "Lord, I believe. Help my unbelief!" Bring healing to my body today, in the name of the Lord Jesus, I pray.

Take the Helmet of Salvation

Heavenly Father, sometimes my mind gets stuck on my present sickness, and I worry. Please be with me as I take the helmet of salvation and put an end to the worrisome thoughts that disturb me. Help me replace thoughts of sickness and defeat with thoughts of healing and hope. Help me see the true value of this vital piece of armor as I stand against sickness and stand for restored health. In Christ's name, amen.

Take Up the Sword of the Spirit

Father God, Almighty Lord, divine Healer, I take up Your sword of the Spirit in fighting this sickness. I rebuke the powers of hell that have laid this sickness on me. I remove the curse of this illness and command it to depart in the name of Jesus Christ, my Lord. Satan, you may not have my body or any part of it. I refuse your symptoms of disease and claim bodily healing for the sake of my Lord and the ministry He's given me. In Jesus's name, I will not spend my days on earth weakened and unable to serve God well. Like the Israelites of old, I will suffer "none of the diseases" [Exodus 15:26]. Thank You, Lord, for Your Word, which brings healing to my body. I receive these words as mine today: "My son, pay attention to what I say; turn your ear to my words. Do not let them out of your sight, keep them within your heart; for they are life to those who find them and health to one's whole body" [Proverbs 4:20-22 NIV]. In Christ's name, amen.

Victory

Pray and ask God to reveal any of your thoughts, beliefs, or words that expose a lack of confidence in your health. Also include anything you have been told by others that may lead you to think that ill health is just a part of life to be expected. Write these all down. For each untruth, look for a countering truth from God's Word. When you write down the countering truth, be sure to cross out the untruth and pray, in Christ's name, that it will no longer affect your life and the lives of those around you. Then thank God that the power of His truth has been let loose to do its work of healing, empowerment, and grace in you. Here's an example.

- *Untruth*: Every year my sinuses get so bad, especially around the change of the seasons.

- *Truth*: "Behold, I will bring to it health and healing, and I will heal them and reveal to them abundance of prosperity and security" (Jeremiah 33:6 ESV).

23

PRAYERS FOR COMFORT

And I will pray the Father, and he shall give you another Comforter, that he may abide with you for ever.

JOHN 14:16 KJV

I wish I could tell you in good conscience that if you come to Jesus, it won't rain on your parade or that you will no longer have to experience difficulties, trials, delays, or other disappointing scenarios. If I could tell you that, I imagine you might shout, clap your hands, and smile big. I would too.

But I can't tell you that simply because it's not true. Yet what I *can* tell you ought to paint a smile on your face, because when you fully grasp this, it will change the way you view life's pain. Here it is: God never allows anything in your life that He does not simultaneously promise to use for good if you are one of His children and living according to His purpose.

If you will make Jesus your focus, He will make His love your comfort and your strength. Place your eyes on Him because He is *for* you. Paul reminds us of the comfort we have as children of God: "Blessed be the God and Father of our Lord Jesus Christ, the Father of mercies and God of all comfort, who comforts us in all our affliction" (2 Corinthians 1:3-4). And Jesus's promise in John 14:16 reminds us that we are not alone.

So I can't say to you that if you come to Jesus or focus on Him, it will never rain. What I *can* say to you is that if you will keep your eyes on Him and His promises in His Word, then when it rains, He will be your covering. He will be your umbrella. He will be the shelter that guards your emotions, your dreams, and the deepest part of who you are. He will protect and nurture that tender part of you that we often refer to as the core or spirit. It's where you feel pain the most.

Jesus will not only cover you but also use the trials and troubles of this life to guide you into your brighter tomorrow. I know that life can hurt. It does hurt. And I know that you may have experienced pain at a level that I cannot identify with. You have been hurt. But rather than allow that hurt to lead you into a path of bitterness, receive the comfort Jesus offers. Take Him at His word. He is with you. You may feel alone, but you are *not* alone. Focus your gaze on the One who promises to cover you with His Spirit. In His covering, you will discover the comfort you need.

Put On the Belt of Truth

I praise You, Lord, for the truth that when I cast my burden on You, You will sustain me [Psalm 55:22]. My burden and pain are a lot to carry around, God. I want to cast them on You and cooperate with this truth as it manifests itself in my life. Show me how to cast my burden on You, Lord, because sometimes I hang on even when I say I have let go. You are "a stronghold for the oppressed, a stronghold in times of trouble" [Psalm 9:9]. I want to experience these truths in my life right now, Lord, so I am accepting them as true and asking You to make them real to me. In Christ's name, amen.

Put On the Breastplate of Righteousness

Lord, I call on Your name right now, just as the psalmist did.

> I love the LORD, because He hears
> My voice and my supplications.

Because He has inclined His ear to me,
Therefore I shall call upon Him as long as I live.
The cords of death encompassed me
And the terrors of Sheol came upon me;
I found distress and sorrow.
Then I called upon the name of the LORD:
"O LORD, I beseech You, save my life!"
Gracious is the LORD, and righteous;
Yes, our God is compassionate.
The LORD preserves the simple;
I was brought low, and He saved me.
Return to your rest, O my soul,
For the LORD has dealt bountifully with you
[Psalm 116:1-7].

Your name and Your graciousness are my comfort and my righteousness, Lord. I pick them up to protect my heart from the effects of this pain. In Christ's name, amen.

Put On the Shoes of Peace

Father, when I am in pain, I feel anything but peace. Instead there is a nagging ache inside of me, longing to be comforted and stilled. I know You tell me to be still and to rest, but I need Your help. I turn to Your Word to help me because I cannot do this on my own. I cannot win this battle on my own. I trust in Your Word:

And I shall lift up my hands to Your commandments,
Which I love;
And I will meditate on Your statutes.
Remember the word to Your servant,
In which You have made me hope.
This is my comfort in my affliction,
That Your word has revived me [Psalm 119:48-50].

In Christ's name, amen.

Take Up the Shield of Faith

Lord, in faith I trust that what I am experiencing right now is not the end of the story. It's not the place where I will wind up. I will laugh again and find joy. I hold up the shield of faith against Satan's accusations that I will not see brighter days. I believe I have a good future. "And he who was seated on the throne said, 'Behold, I am making all things new.' Also He said, 'Write this down, for these words are trustworthy and true'" [Revelation 21:5 ESV]. Your Word also says, "Weeping may tarry for the night, but joy comes with the morning" [Psalm 30:5 ESV]. In faith, I trust that morning has come and You will fill me with joy. In Christ's name, amen.

Take the Helmet of Salvation

Heavenly Father, "It is of the LORD's mercies that we are not consumed, because his compassions fail not. They are new every morning: great is thy faithfulness" [Lamentations 3:22-23 KJV]. The faithfulness of Your mercy keeps my mind right and sets my heart on a pathway to healing. I trust not only in Your eternal salvation, Father, but also in Your salvation from my present pain and suffering. Give me the comfort I need to brave this day, this night, and to receive Your joy. In Christ's name, amen.

Take Up the Sword of the Spirit

Father God, it is written, "Be of sober spirit, be on the alert. Your adversary, the devil, prowls around like a roaring lion, seeking someone to devour" [1 Peter 5:8]. I am alert to the devil's schemes. He tempts me to focus on feelings of hopelessness in the midst of my pain. But this is the offensive weapon I take to Satan right now: "The LORD is good, a stronghold in the day of trouble, and He knows those who take refuge in Him" [Nahum 1:7]. Thank You for assuring me that You know me. I take refuge in You. In Christ's name, amen.

Victory

Pray and ask God to reveal any unhelpful thoughts, beliefs, or words that show a resignation to your pain, a spirit of giving up, or a victim mentality. Also consider things you have heard in the media or from friends and family that cause you to feel alone in your pain, to feel as if there is no hope for a better tomorrow. Write these all down. For each untruth, look for a countering truth from God's Word. When you write down the countering truth, be sure to cross out the untruth and pray, in Christ's name, that it will no longer affect your life and the lives of those around you. Then thank God that the power of His truth has been let loose to do its work of healing, empowerment, and grace in you. Here's an example.

- *Untruth*: My heart is an open sore.
- *Truth*: "He heals the brokenhearted and binds up their wounds" (Psalm 147:3).

24

PRAYING FOR MY CHILDREN

*I have chosen him, so that he may command his children
and his household after him to keep the way of the LORD
by doing righteousness and justice, so that the LORD may
bring upon Abraham what He has spoken about him.*

GENESIS 18:19

Families determine the future, making parenting one of the most critical tasks on earth. Yet Satan has steadily dismantled the family. Satan despises the family because God has chosen to bless the earth through the family. Parents have been placed here by God to counteract Satan's schemes, and one way we are to do that is by instructing our kids in God's Word.

Many of our children are not growing up and living out their destinies because they have been raised with a mindset that mirrors the culture. It is me-centered. But if you accept the culture's god, or if you turn yourself into a god, you forfeit the one, true God. He won't share His glory with anyone else. Too many of our kids are being raised without an understanding of God's Word, so they fail to apply it to their lives. That is not the kids' fault. That responsibility rests squarely on the shoulders of the parents.

Raising kingdom kids includes more than taking your kids to Sunday school. It involves introducing them repeatedly to the King of kings and Lord of lords. Teaching them that God is highly exalted and reigns supreme. Giving them a kingdom perspective to realize that they must submit all of their life to God's comprehensive rule. Reminding them that God's Word is the law of the land. When they live according to that perspective, they are positioned to experience the fullness of life Christ died to give.

In addition to the prayers written below, your warfare for your children focuses on their protection, the wisdom they will gain, the calling of God on their lives, and your stewardship as a parent.

Put On the Belt of Truth

Lord, You are a Father—a parent—so You understand how I feel when my children go astray. When my children don't walk in truth, but walk in darkness under the influence of the enemy, I reach out to You, asking You to help me guide them into truth. I pray my children will see the lies of the enemy for what they are—a GPS for the way to hell and destruction. Lord, empower me as a parent to lead well, to love even better, and to give my children ears to hear what is true and to discern between right and wrong. In Christ's name, amen.

Put On the Breastplate of Righteousness

Father, You are holy and righteous. There is no unrighteousness in You. Thank You for giving me Christ's righteousness as my own. I wear righteousness as a breastplate—a piece of armor against the schemes of the enemy. I pray that You would put a hunger for righteousness in my children. You have said, "Blessed are those who hunger and thirst for righteousness, for they will be filled" [Matthew 5:6 NIV]. I pray for my children to hunger desperately for the righteousness that comes from trusting You. Lord, hear my prayer! In Christ's name, amen.

Put On the Shoes of Peace

God, I worry about my children, but You would have me be at peace. You would have me put on the shoes of peace as part of my armor against the schemes of the enemy. I do put on those shoes today and walk in peace, trusting that You love my children even more than I do. I trust that You will do whatever it takes to bring my children into a loving and deep relationship with You. Help my children to find peace, and help me to make our home peaceful on all levels. Forgive me for allowing conflict to enter and remain. In Christ's name, amen.

Take Up the Shield of Faith

Today, Father in heaven, I take up the shield of faith on behalf of my children. I war against the forces of hell that seek to take my children captive. In faith, I refuse to allow Satan to continue harassing and toying with my children. I pray today for the influence of Your Holy Spirit in my children. By faith I ask You to surround them with Your angels of protection, shielding them from the enemy's schemes in their hearts and minds. I believe that You have put a divine call on their lives. I pray for that calling to be evident to my children early in life. I pray today against the lies of the culture that would try to shape my children in its image—the image of the evil one. I pray instead that my children would follow You and be changed from glory to glory into Your likeness. God, put a desire for You in the heart of my children. In Christ's name, amen.

Take the Helmet of Salvation

O Lord, I praise You for Your salvation. You save us from our sins and from our enemy. In Your salvation, the enemy has no position of influence, no ground to accuse or intimidate. Lord, bring Your eternal salvation into the lives of my children. Sanctify them by Your power on a daily basis. Influence them to seek You in earnest. In Christ's name, I silence the enemy of their future and their hope. I set a wall of protection around my children—a wall the enemy cannot penetrate. Lord, pour out Your love on my children in such an irresistible way that they are brought to tears over Your mercy and tender care. In Christ's name, amen.

Take Up the Sword of the Spirit

Father God, I take up the sword of the Spirit in the fight for my children. I declare that no satanic weapon will prosper against them. In the name of Jesus Christ, who died for my children, I put a stop to all of the enemy's influences on them. I rebuke the enemy's hold on their minds and release them from it. I hold them up before Your throne, O Lord, and intercede in Christ's name for total healing and restoration. Bring my children home, Lord. It is written, "Train up a child in the way he should go, even when he is old he will not depart from it" [Proverbs 22:6]. I claim this truth right now for the present and the future. In Christ's name, amen.

Victory

Pray and ask God to reveal any of your thoughts, beliefs, or words that are not aligned with God's will or plans for your children. Maybe you said or thought these things because you were frustrated with them or with yourself. Write these all down. For each untruth, look for a countering truth from God's Word. When you write down the countering truth, be sure to cross out the untruth and pray, in Christ's name, that it will no longer affect your life and the lives of those around you. Then thank God that the power of His truth has been let loose to do its work of healing, empowerment, and grace in you. Here's an example.

- *Untruth*: I lose my temper because they frustrate me.
- *Truth*: "Fathers, do not exasperate your children, so that they will not lose heart" (Colossians 3:21).

25

DELIVERANCE FROM SEXUAL STRONGHOLDS

This is the will of God, your sanctification;
that is, that you abstain from sexual immorality.

1 THESSALONIANS 4:3

God invented sex. But Satan has distorted it just as he has many of God's other great delights, perverting sexuality to the extent that it has become an addiction and stronghold for many men and women, including Christians. However, through the power of the Holy Spirit, deliverance from sexual strongholds is possible. As with many other strongholds, continued prayer and ongoing warfare may be necessary. Prayer, faith, walking out our deliverance by adopting healthy sexual attitudes…these are some of the keys to victory.

Sexual strongholds may be more difficult to overcome than many other strongholds because sexual strongholds don't always show up in the physical world. For instance, people can have a sexual stronghold and never actually engage in sex. Instead, their sexual stronghold may manifest itself through an addiction to pornography, fantasizing, or achieving personal gratification through illegitimate means contrary to God's plan for sex. Thinking about alcohol doesn't make people drunk. Thinking about cocaine doesn't make people high. But thinking about sex is often its own fulfillment.

People who would never do anything wrong sexually often find as much satisfaction in the thought as they would in the action. Jesus says, "I tell you that anyone who looks at a woman lustfully has already committed adultery with her in his heart" (Matthew 5:28 NIV). When God views a sexual stronghold, He doesn't just view the physical.

Put On the Belt of Truth

Father, thank You for the gift of sex. I pray that I can see the truth about sex as You intended it. The belt of truth about sexuality will guard me from the false notions society tries to engrain in my mind—that sex is just recreational, with no responsibility or consequences attached to it. For that reason, I daily put on the belt of truth about the proper place sexual desire has in my life. In Christ's name, amen.

Put On the Breastplate of Righteousness

Lord, there is righteousness in sex the way You planned it. The marriage bed is undefiled. Sexual unrighteousness has no place among Your people and thus no place in my life. I put on the breastplate of righteousness to guard me against the unrighteous pull of sex beyond the borders of Your intentions for sexual pleasure. In Christ's name, amen.

Put On the Shoes of Peace

Daily, Lord, I put on the shoes of Your peace. The conflict in my flesh over sexual desire is put at ease with true peace. I watch where my feet take me as I wear the shoes of peace. Likewise, I guard what I look at, and with David I vow that "I will set nothing wicked before my eyes" [Psalm 101:3 NKJV]. In Christ's name, amen.

Take Up the Shield of Faith

Father, daily I'm confronted with sexual images all around me that tempt me to sin. With each such image, I raise high the shield of faith to repel those tempting thoughts lest they take root in my imagination and lead me to sin physically or in my heart. Lord, thank You for that effective shield against the pornographic arrows of the enemy. In Christ's name, amen.

Take the Helmet of Salvation

God, even without the world's provocative images tempting me, my own mind conjures up illicit thoughts that propel me toward sin. But to protect my thought life, You have given me a helmet—the helmet of salvation that literally saves me from sexual sin as those thoughts take no root in my mind. Thank You for this great helmet, which is effective 24/7—the hours I need it most. In Christ's name, amen.

Take Up the Sword of the Spirit

Lord, sexual immorality is Satan's perversion of Your gift of sex. With the sword of the Spirit, I cut down the enemy's evil thoughts and replace them with Your Word, which purifies me. No temptation can stand when I wield the sword. It cuts through the enemy's designs every time. This sword is always ready for the battle, and daily it's my defense and offense against sinful sexual imaginations. In Christ's name, amen.

Victory

Pray and ask God to reveal any of your thoughts, beliefs, or words that reflect false notions about sexuality or a corrupted viewpoint on God's purpose for sex. Write these all down. For each untruth, look for a countering truth from God's Word. When you write down the countering truth, be sure to cross out the untruth and pray, in Christ's name, that it will no longer affect your life and the lives of those around you. Then thank God that the power of His truth has been let loose to do its work of healing, empowerment, and grace in you. Here's an example.

- *Untruth*: Immoral sex isn't all that bad as long as I use precautions.

- *Truth*: "Flee from sexual immorality. Every other sin a person commits is outside the body, but the sexually immoral person sins against his own body" (1 Corinthians 6:18 ESV).

26

OPENING MY EYES

Elisha prayed and said, "O LORD, I pray, open his eyes that he may see." And the LORD opened the servant's eyes and he saw; and behold, the mountain was full of horses and chariots of fire all around Elisha.

2 KINGS 6:17

I love the heat. I was born up north in Baltimore, but I got to Dallas as quickly as I could. My wife, Lois, and I moved to Dallas in the 1970s so I could attend seminary, and when we did, I discovered a benefit about Dallas—the heat. Dallas is known for its heat.

Another great thing about Dallas is the immensity of the Texas sky. Sometimes it seems as if you can look straight into eternity when you look at the Texas sky.

An interesting thing happened the other night as I looked at the sky around dusk. I saw one lone star in the enormous expanse, but the rest of the sky appeared empty. A few minutes later, I looked again. This time the sky had gotten a little darker, and so I saw a couple of stars. A few minutes later, I looked again. More stars. The stars reminded me of a spiritual truth that ought to be part of your prayers for victory in spiritual warfare: All of the stars were already in place when I looked up that very first time. I couldn't see them, but they had been there all along.

I want you to remember that God has already given you everything you need to fight and win your spiritual battle. It is already inside you. When you placed your faith in Christ for the forgiveness of your sins, you received the full impartation of the Holy Spirit within you. You received access to the authority you need to defeat the enemy.

But realizing that you have that access might be another story. Sometimes we need help seeing clearly, and that's why spiritual warfare includes praying that God will open your eyes to see things spiritually in much the same way that He opened the eyes of the servant in response to the prophet's prayer.

Put On the Belt of Truth

Lord, the first place for me to start in opening my eyes spiritually is in Your Word. "For the word of God is living and active, sharper than any two-edged sword, piercing to the division of soul and of spirit, of joints and of marrow, and discerning the thoughts and intentions of the heart" [Hebrews 4:12 ESV]. Thank You for Your Word, which gives me discernment into my own life. It gives me the ability to look beyond the physical world and to see the spiritual root behind the issues I face. In Christ's name, amen.

Put On the Breastplate of Righteousness

Lord God, I put on the breastplate of righteousness so that I might rightly discern what is happening around me. I do not wrestle against flesh and blood. If I think that people are my problem, I will focus on them and completely miss the actual root of the problem. The people are real. The problems are real. The health issues are real. The challenges are real. The conflicts are real. The strongholds are real. But they are not the root. Satan and his demons would keep me from experiencing the abundant life You have in store for me. They would distract me from the spiritual root behind the issue I am facing. I choose to look rightly to You, Lord, to show me this root. In Christ's name, amen.

Put On the Shoes of Peace

Father, when the servant saw only the approaching army, he no doubt felt afraid. Peace was probably the furthest thing from his mind. Yet when Elisha prayed for his eyes to be opened to see Your army, You gave him peace and confidence. I want the same, Lord. I ask that You will open my eyes to see not only the nature of the battles I face but also Your victorious angels and the way You will overcome. In Christ's name, amen.

Take Up the Shield of Faith

Lord, I take up the shield of faith against the issues I face, knowing that without faith it is impossible to please You. Yet when I come to You in faith, You will reward me. Faith means I can't always see everything. I need to believe Your Word, sometimes in spite of what I see. That's faith. And then I need to act on that belief. This is the shield I carry with me to fight off Satan's fiery darts that entice me to cower and sin. In Christ's name, amen.

Take the Helmet of Salvation

O Lord, my God, it is easy to feel insecure when I don't have the spiritual vantage point that You have from the heavenlies. When I look at things and discern them through my five senses, I can forget Your great victory in securing my salvation. Through my salvation You have also secured my victory in spiritual warfare, and for that I thank You. Help me to have Your viewpoint continually so I can rest. In Christ's name, amen.

Take Up the Sword of the Spirit

Father, I have been born again through faith in Jesus Christ, so I am not a natural person operating in the flesh. It is written, "The natural person does not accept the things of the Spirit of God, for they are folly to him, and he is not able to understand them because they are spiritually discerned" [1 Corinthians 2:14 ESV]. Father, give me ears to hear You and eyes to see spiritually so I can know how to pray, what to ask for, and how to seek Your name regarding the issues I face in my life. In Christ's name, amen.

Victory

Pray and ask God to reveal any of your thoughts, beliefs, or words that reflect a tangible, physical viewpoint of the problems you face. Write these all down. For each untruth, look for a countering truth from God's Word. When you write down the countering truth, be sure to cross out the untruth and pray, in Christ's name, that it will no longer affect your life and the lives of those around you. Then thank God that the power of His truth has been let loose to do its work of healing, empowerment, and grace in you. Here's an example.

- *Untruth*: My boss/coworker gets on my every last nerve, and I don't know how to work well with him/her.

- *Truth*: "If any of you lacks wisdom, let him ask God, who gives generously to all without reproach, and it will be given him" (James 1:5 ESV).

27

GUARDING MY TONGUE

The tongue is a fire, the very world of iniquity; the tongue is
set among our members as that which defiles the entire body,
and sets on fire the course of our life, and is set on fire by hell.

JAMES 3:6

I am amazed at how much the Bible says about our speech. If you want to do a study that will challenge and change you, check out God's Word on your words. Proverbs 10:19 says, "When there are many words, transgression is unavoidable, but he who restrains his lips is wise." According to Proverbs 12:22, "Lying lips are an abomination to the LORD." And Proverbs 15:1 tells us, "A gentle answer turns away wrath, but a harsh word stirs up anger."

We could go on and on. The Bible's advice about our words can be summed up in the phrase, "Be quick to hear [and] slow to speak" (James 1:19). God wants us to weigh and measure our words and make sure they are aimed in the right direction before we let them fly.

We'd better make sure we know where our words are taking us because we follow our words as surely as a horse obeys its rider or a ship is guided by its rudder (James 3:3-4). We need to understand how our words cause us problems and why taming the tongue is so hard.

James gets us started. "The tongue is a small part of the body, and yet it boasts of great things. See how great a forest is set aflame by such a small fire!" (3:5). We all know that a single ember from a fireplace can burn down an entire house. One lone match can take out a huge forest.

The Bible uses the powerful imagery of fire to illustrate the perversity of the tongue and its ability to set things aflame.

Many married people wish they could take back words spoken in anger or frustration, words that burned their mates with fire that is still smoldering. Some believers have started gossip fires that consumed someone's reputation. (Remember, a person who will gossip to you will certainly gossip about you.) Being more like Jesus means using our tongue, despite its perversity and with the help of the Holy Spirit, to refresh others rather than rip them apart.

Proverbs 10:11 says, "The mouth of the righteous is a fountain of life." According to Proverbs 13:14, "The teaching of the wise is a fountain of life." The difference between the right word and the wrong word is the difference between a life-giving fountain and a bone-dry riverbed.

How can we win the spiritual battle for our tongues? We begin by giving God the ever-important control of our tongues. How do we do that? Through prayer. Why not make this prayer from God's Word your own? "Set a guard, O Lord, over my mouth; keep watch over the door of my lips" (Psalm 141:3).

Put On the Belt of Truth

Lord, may my tongue be a vessel of Your truth. I take the truth of Your Word as my belt, girding me for battle. Let my speech be flavored with Your love and compassion. Give me Your words of truth to speak today. Your truth tells me that "death and life are in the power of the tongue, and those who love it will eat its fruit" [Proverbs 18:21]. Lord, I confess that I have seen death in my own life due to my own tongue. I repent and ask You to raise the dead where I have brought death and restore the relationships I have ruined by my words. In Christ's name, amen.

Put On the Breastplate of Righteousness

Father, as I put on the breastplate of righteousness, may my tongue be a fountain of righteousness. Guard my tongue, Lord, against all unrighteousness. I have read in Your Word, "I tell you, on the day of judgment people will give account for every careless word they speak, for by your words you will be justified, and by your words you will be condemned" [Matthew 12:36-37 ESV.] My righteousness or unrighteousness is on display in my words. The tongue is a temperature gauge revealing whether I am walking in a right spirit with You. Guard my tongue, God, that I might live in righteousness before You. In Christ's name, amen.

Put On the Shoes of Peace

Lord, fill me with Your Spirit—from my mouth and tongue to the bottom of my feet. As I put on the shoes of peace, I pray that my words would always convey messages of peace. Fill me today with Your Spirit and order my steps in peace. You have said, "Let no corrupting talk come out of your mouths, but only such as is good for building up, as fits the occasion, that it may give grace to those who hear" [Ephesians 4:29 ESV]. When my words give grace, Lord, peace reigns in my relationships and in my own heart. In Christ's name, amen.

Take Up the Shield of Faith

Lord, I pray for the shield of faith operating in my life today as I speak Your truth. Keep me from speaking faithless words to myself or to others. Teach me, Lord, to walk and talk in faith. I pick up the shield of faith against the accusations of Satan. His accusations are real. I have sinned with my tongue. I have ruined relationships and hurt others with what I have said. And yet I pick up the shield of faith that says, "If we confess our sins, he is faithful and just to forgive us our sins and to cleanse us from all unrighteousness" [1 John 1:9 ESV]. With this shield I trust that I am forgiven and that the same power that raised Jesus from the dead can mend, heal, and restore relationships where my tongue has brought ruin. I believe this and thank You ahead of time, God. In Christ's name, amen.

Take the Helmet of Salvation

Heavenly Father, as I wear the helmet of salvation today, may I speak as a saved person should. Put a guard over my lips so that I can easily speak words of salvation and faith. Convict me when I speak like someone who doesn't have the helmet of salvation.

Take Up the Sword of the Spirit

O Lord, my tongue can be unruly sometimes. When that happens today, I pray You'll remind me of the mighty sword of the Spirit, which is the Word of God. Bring to my remembrance Scriptures that fit the moment perfectly. By the Spirit of God, may my tongue be tamed, controlled, and entrusted with Your words of life. Satan, through the power of Jesus Christ, I remove your influence on my thoughts and my tongue. I will not speak negativity, doubt, or criticism to those I meet today because, as it is written, "A word fitly spoken is like apples of gold in a setting of silver" [Proverbs 25:11 ESV].

Victory

Pray and ask God to reveal any of your thoughts, beliefs, or words that are wrong, negative, hurtful, and damaging. Also consider things others may have said to you. Write these all down. For each untruth, look for a countering truth from God's Word. When you write down the countering truth, be sure to cross out the untruth and pray, in Christ's name, that it will no longer affect your life and the lives of those around you. Then thank God that the power of His truth has been let loose to do its work of healing, empowerment, and grace in you. Here's an example.

- *Untruth*: Republicans/Democrats are stupid.
- *Truth*: "Let there be no filthiness nor foolish talk nor crude joking, which are out of place, but instead let there be thanksgiving" (Ephesians 5:4 ESV).

28

OVERCOMING ENVY

*Let us not become boastful, challenging
one another, envying one another.*

GALATIANS 5:26

You will find very few people today who are content. Our culture of advertising and marketing always dangles another carrot in order to get us to want more, spend more, and do more. With the ease of technology at our fingers, we can spend, spend, spend like never before. With just one click, whatever you're looking at on your computer screen can arrive on your doorstep the next day. It's difficult to remain content when you are continually being told what else you need in order to make yourself happy, healthy, or attractive.

Paul called the art of being satisfied, or overcoming envy, a secret. We read, "I know how to get along with humble means, and I also know how to live in prosperity; in any and every circumstance I have learned the secret of being filled and going hungry, both of having abundance and suffering need" (Philippians 4:12).

Paul spoke of true contentment. It means to have access to the resources you need in order to handle whatever it is you are dealing with. In other words, you have enough for what you need at any given time, whether that is a lot or a little.

How do you know when you are content? Contentment means being

151

at rest, thankful, and grateful for whatever situation you find yourself in. You can always know people's contentment level by whether they are usually complaining or being grateful. If complaints are constant, there is no contentment. If words of gratitude predominate, contentment is there.

Paul's secret will give you victory over envy if you will learn and apply it. Life has ebbs and flows. Sometimes you are up financially, and sometimes things will be tight. There will always be someone who has more money than you, more skills, better looks...you name it. You will enjoy victory in spiritual warfare over envy when Paul's secret rules your heart and mind, when you value what is most important in life—your relationships with God and with others.

Put On the Belt of Truth

Lord, You are my perfect Father. You provide for all my needs. In putting on the belt of truth, I acknowledge Your care for me. I have no need to envy or covet what someone else has. I bless You, God, for what You've given them, and I'm content with what You've given me. The truth is, when I seek first You and Your kingdom, You make sure I have everything I need [Matthew 6:33]. Thank You, God, that I can rest in this truth. In Christ's name, amen.

Put On the Breastplate of Righteousness

Father, today I put on the breastplate of righteousness in my desire not to covet what others have. You have given me the righteousness of Christ, which was not mine, but a gift from You. Likewise, everything else You give me is a gift that I receive with contentment and gratitude. Contentment carries with it a certain righteousness and will protect me in spiritual warfare. Your Word says, "Godliness with contentment is great gain, for we brought nothing into the world, and we cannot take anything out of the world. But if we have food and clothing, with these we will be content" [1 Timothy 6:6-8 ESV]. Help me to maintain that attitude. In Christ's name, amen.

Put On the Shoes of Peace

Lord, as I put on the shoes of peace today, I experience the peace of knowing You are meeting all my needs. In peace, I don't strive for anything that isn't from Your hand. I rejoice with others in Your abundance to them and to me. Thank You, Lord. In Christ's name, amen.

Take Up the Shield of Faith

Father, by faith I thank You for being the supplier of all my needs. I refuse the accusations of the enemy that cause me to covet what others have. Satan, you have tempted me with a desire for things God may not want me to have. I refuse to listen to your deceitful charge that God doesn't supply everything He should. My hope is in God alone because I have faith that when I hope in Him, I will not be disappointed [Psalm 25:3 NIV]. In Christ's name, amen.

Take the Helmet of Salvation

God, thank You for the helmet of salvation. With this piece of armor I guard myself against the lies of the enemy. I am saved from the world and the devil, rescued from the domain of darkness, and transferred to the kingdom of Your beloved Son [Colossians 1:13], where there is no want. Give me this day my daily bread, Lord, and I am content. In Christ's name, amen.

Take Up the Sword of the Spirit

Lord, I take up the sword of the Spirit and declare my needs met by Your unseen hand [Philippians 4:19]. You will give me what I need, so I have no desire to covet or envy what another person has. Satan, I cast down your evil thoughts that God has failed to meet my needs. The Word is my sword, my weapon against the enemy. I read in Luke 12:15 [ESV], "Take care, and be on your guard against all covetousness, for one's life does not consist in the abundance of his possessions." My life does not consist of my possessions. In Christ's name, amen.

Victory

Pray and ask God to bring to light any of your thoughts, beliefs, or words that reveal a heart of spirit of envy. Also note anything you may have in you that resembles complaining or ingratitude. Write these all down. For each untruth, look for a countering truth from God's Word. When you write down the countering truth, be sure to cross out the untruth and pray, in Christ's name, that it will no longer affect your life and the lives of those around you. Then thank God that the power of His truth has been let loose to do its work of healing, empowerment, and grace in you. Here's an example.

- *Untruth*: I need a new car.

- *Truth*: "Godliness with contentment is great gain, for we brought nothing into the world, and we cannot take anything out of the world. But if we have food and clothing, with these we will be content. But those who desire to be rich fall into temptation, into a snare, into many senseless and harmful desires that plunge people into ruin and destruction. For the love of money is a root of all kinds of evils" (1 Timothy 6:6-8 ESV).

29

WHEN I AM WEARY

He gives strength to the weary,
And to him who lacks might He increases power.

ISAIAH 40:29

If you are like most of us who multitask, juggle multiple things at once, and try to spin several plates all at the same time, you know what it is like to feel exhausted, weary, and weighed down by a heavy burden. Being weary is different from being sleepy. You can usually fix sleepiness with a good night's sleep or a nap in an easy chair. But weariness dictates how you will feel and what you will do. Being weary means you can no longer relax. Being weary means you are no longer able to be at home with who you are. You have lost your peace.

If this describes you, I have good news for you. Jesus offers freedom from what weighs you down. This freedom comes through one of the greatest words in Scripture—"rest." Jesus says He has come to give you rest. He gives you a place to dock. He gives you a way to be rid of the worries and cares you drag through life. He promises rest from your labors in heaven as well as ongoing rest while you're still here on earth. He says, "Come to Me, all who are weary and heavy-laden, and I will give you rest. Take my yoke upon you and learn from Me, for I am gentle and humble in heart, and you will find rest for your souls" (Matthew 11:28-29).

Jesus tells us that we can replace our burdens with His yoke. He says that if we yoke up with Him and learn from Him, we will find the rest we so desperately crave. We will find the freedom we need. We will find refreshment. Remember Martha and Mary? Jesus scolded Martha because she tried to do so much all at once that she became frustrated and began complaining. But Mary had chosen the better thing—to sit at Jesus's feet, where she was released from the bondage of weariness and able to soak in what mattered most.

God wants to release you from weariness too. He wants you to experience the fullness of the life He has in store for you, which includes rest.

Put On the Belt of Truth

Father, I get so weary. I need Your truth to be my belt at such times. I claim Your promise in Isaiah 40:31:

> Those who wait for the LORD
> Will gain new strength;
> They will mount up with wings like eagles,
> They will run and not get tired,
> They will walk and not become weary.

Lord, help me to mount up with wings of eagles! In Christ's name, amen.

Put On the Breastplate of Righteousness

Heavenly Father, living in unrighteousness is so tiring. I thank You for the refreshment of righteousness, which I wear as a breastplate against unreasonable weariness. Thank You, God, for new strength. Forgive me for piling up my schedule with too many things—even good things. I pray for discernment to choose not just what is good, but what is best. Help me to do right in getting enough rest. In Christ's name, amen.

Put On the Shoes of Peace

Walking a long way is hard, Lord. My feet get tired of walking through each day. But You have given me new shoes. Shoes that are part of my divine armor. Shoes of peace. I praise You, Lord, for strengthening me to walk the extra mile in the durable shoes of peace. And thank You for times when I can take off my shoes and simply be in Your presence, Lord. When I abide in You, You fight my battles for me and carry my burdens. You even provide for me while I sleep.

> It is vain for you to rise up early,
> To retire late,
> To eat the bread of painful labors;
> For He gives to His beloved even in his sleep [Psalm 127:2].

Take Up the Shield of Faith

Father, I've noticed that when my faith is low, my strength is also low. I pray for a fresh infusion of divine strength as I raise the shield of faith. Lord, don't let any of the work You've called me to do suffer for my lack of strength or weak faith. In Christ's name, amen.

Take the Helmet of Salvation

God, I take up the helmet of salvation, for in Your salvation there is new life and new strength. Lord, help me be full of energy today, and let none of it be wasted. In Christ's name, amen.

Take Up the Sword of the Spirit

Lord, I know when I'm weary from overwork, overserving, or overscheduling, I become vulnerable, setting myself up as a target for the enemy. I take up the sword of the Spirit and cut off Satan's ability to make me feel weary. I take back my calendar, trusting that You are my provider and my source. You are the strength of my life [Psalm 27:1 NKJV], and You release me from any unreasonable tiredness or weariness that Satan would try to put on me. You have given me strength for each of my days [Deuteronomy 33:25 NKJV]. Praise You! In Christ's name, amen.

Victory

Pray and ask God to reveal any of your thoughts, beliefs, or words that indicate your heart is weary. Write these all down. For each untruth, look for a countering truth from God's Word. When you write down the countering truth, be sure to cross out the untruth and pray, in Christ's name, that it will no longer affect your life and the lives of those around you. Then thank God that the power of His truth has been let loose to do its work of healing, empowerment, and grace in you. Here's an example.

- *Untruth*: I'll never get through this.

- *Truth*: "God is able to make all grace abound to you, so that always having all sufficiency in everything, you may have an abundance for every good deed" (2 Corinthians 9:8).

30

PRAYERS FOR PERSECUTED CHRISTIANS AROUND THE WORLD

*They overcame him because of the blood of the Lamb
and because of the word of their testimony, and they
did not love their life even when faced with death.*

REVELATION 12:11

It's no surprise that Satan hates Christians and schemes to render them powerless or remove them from the battlefield. As he plots against believers, using anti-Christian leaders or terrorist groups to destroy the faithful, he sees victory ahead.

But as we pray for our persecuted brothers and sisters around the world, Satan's power to destroy the global church is held back. Never give up praying for the persecuted church. One way to pray is to ask God to lay a specific country on your heart and then faithfully pray daily for the Christians of that country. Pray too for that country's leaders.

Another way to pray is to follow Christ's example in the Lord's Prayer, praying for God's kingdom to come and His will to be done on earth as it is in heaven. When you pray for the advancement of God's kingdom, you are praying in accordance with the will of God. Only God knows how He can use something so evil as the persecution of Christians to expand His kingdom, so we do not always know what to pray. But when we ask Him to turn what was intended for evil into good, we leave the situation in His hands and trust Him to carry out His attack on the enemy.

As you pray, always remember to cover yourself with the blood of Jesus Christ, which protects us from the enemy. Satan wants you to fight in your own strength and power, but when you are covered in Christ's blood, you have the strength and protection you need to wage this war well. Develop a habit of intentionally praying for Christ's covering in this way because the battles you are waging in the heavenlies are brutal, and you need to be under Christ to fully live out your victory and to pray that persecuted Christians around the world can fully live out theirs.

Put On the Belt of Truth

Lord, wherever Your truth is preached, the enemy is close behind to attack with lies and accusations. Today I put on the belt of truth, praying that my fellow Christians around the world will boldly continue to preach and live out Your gospel. Lord, may the enemy be exposed for what he is—the father of lies. I pray You'll give safety and blessing to Christians who fear for their lives. Strengthen them in the faith and embolden them with Your Holy Spirit. In Christ's name, amen.

Put On the Breastplate of Righteousness

Father, wherever the gospel goes, righteousness goes. When light comes in, darkness flees. I put on the breastplate of righteousness today, praying on behalf of suffering brothers and sisters around the world. Lord, give them courage and strength to stand for righteousness in the face of persecution. As for me, I too need this breastplate as I stand up for Your gospel in my circle of influence. Father, I pray You would give great boldness to Your church around the world. In our nation, Lord, help us to live in righteousness as we come under attack. I lift up our spiritual leaders and ask that You will help them to live in righteousness, convicting and correcting them when they are wrong. In Christ's name, amen.

Put On the Shoes of Peace

O Lord, how hard it is to wear the shoes of peace when so many of my fellow believers are suffering violence. Their lives are in upheaval because of their faith in You. I pray for them, Lord, and I ask for peace for them and for me. I put on the shoes of peace even as I continue to intercede for them. God, bring peace to them. Bring relief from the enemy's onslaught against them. Bring peace to the communities in our nation as well, Lord, that suffer under the chaos of injustice—racial discrimination, class wars, financial corruption, and so much more. In Christ's name, amen.

Take Up the Shield of Faith

Today, I take up the shield of faith in my battle for the safety and faith of persecuted Christians around the world. In faith, I come against the satanic forces aimed against believers in foreign lands and here at home. By faith, Lord, I ask You to come to their aid. Give them courage and a strong heart. I plead the blood of Christ over the ones Satan is viciously attacking around the world. I cast down every effort to destroy them or to coerce them to deny their faith. These believers are precious in Your sight, and their reward in heaven is great. Satan has no right to them, and I hold high the banner of faith against his harassment of them. In Christ's name, amen.

Take the Helmet of Salvation

Father, thank You for Your salvation! Thank You for saving me. Wearing the helmet of my salvation, I pray for those whose salvation is costing them their homes, their livelihood, and even their lives. Lord, I intercede for them. Lift their burden, Father. Bring them springs of living water to refresh them. Let them know that they're not forgotten and that others are praying for them. In Christ's name, amen.

Take Up the Sword of the Spirit

Lord, I take up the sword of the Spirit to battle on behalf of those who are suffering for Your name's sake. Your Word breaks the bonds of the captives, Lord, and I pray Your Word for these persecuted ones. You have said, "Blessed are those who have been persecuted for the sake of righteousness, for theirs is the kingdom of heaven" [Matthew 5:10]. So, Lord, for those who are persecuted, I pray a blessing from You—not just in eternity but also here and now. Bless them, Lord, for their faithfulness. Satan, you cannot have those who belong to the Lord. In Christ's name, you must release your hold on them. According to God's Word, these people are blessed, and you cannot take away that blessing. I rebuke your work against God's beloved children. I cast away your lies to them that they have been forgotten or abandoned. I pray for supernatural faith and strength as they continue in faithfulness in spite of your efforts to destroy them. God, please bless them, even beyond what they hope or think. In Christ's name, amen.

Victory

Pray and ask God to reveal any of your thoughts, beliefs, or words that reveal a spirit of apathy for believers in the body of Christ who are being persecuted. Also consider ways your attitudes or actions show your concern for self-preservation rather than concern for your brothers and sisters in Christ. Write these all down. For each untruth, look for a countering truth from God's Word. When you write down the countering truth, be sure to cross out the untruth and pray, in Christ's name, that it will no longer affect your life and the lives of those around you. Then thank God that the power of His truth has been let loose to do its work of healing, empowerment, and grace in you. Here's an example.

- *Untruth*: It's not essential to always reveal that you are a Christian—not when harm might come.
- *Truth*: "If anyone suffers as a Christian, let him not be ashamed, but let him glorify God in that name" (1 Peter 4:16 ESV).

About Dr. Tony Evans

Dr. Tony Evans is founder and senior pastor of Oak Cliff Bible Fellowship in Dallas, founder and president of The Urban Alternative, chaplain of the NBA's Dallas Mavericks, and author of *The Power of God's Names*, *Victory in Spiritual Warfare*, and many other books. His radio broadcast, *The Alternative with Dr. Tony Evans*, can be heard on more than 1000 US outlets daily and in more than 130 countries.

THE URBAN ALTERNATIVE

Dr. Evans and The Urban Alternative (TUA) equip, empower, and unite Christians to impact *individuals, families, churches,* and *communities,* restoring hope and transforming lives.

We believe the core cause of the problems we face in our personal lives, homes, churches, and societies is a spiritual one. Therefore, the only way to address them is spiritually. We've tried political, social, economic, and even religious agendas. It's time for a kingdom agenda—God's visible and comprehensive rule over every area of life—because when we function as we were designed, God's divine power changes everything. It renews and restores as the life of Christ is made manifest in our own. As we align ourselves under Him, He brings about full restoration from deep within. In this atmosphere, people are revived and made whole.

As God's kingdom impacts us, it impacts others—transforming every sphere of life. When each sphere of life functions in accordance with God's Word, the outcomes are evangelism, discipleship, and community impact. As we learn how to govern ourselves under God, we transform the institutions of family, church, and society according to a biblically based kingdom perspective. Through Him, we are touching heaven and changing earth.

To achieve our goal, we use a variety of strategies, methods, and resources for reaching and equipping as many people as possible.

Broadcast Media

Hundreds of thousands of individuals experience *The Alternative with Dr. Tony Evans* through daily radio broadcasts on more than 1000 radio outlets and in more than 130 countries. The broadcast can also be seen on several television networks and online at TonyEvans.org.

Leadership Training

Kingdom Agenda Pastors (KAP) provides a viable network for like-minded pastors who embrace the kingdom agenda philosophy. Pastors have the opportunity to go deeper with Dr. Evans as they are given biblical knowledge, practical applications, and resources to impact individuals, families, churches, and communities. KAP welcomes senior and associate pastors of all churches.

Kingdom Agenda Pastors' Summit progressively develops church leaders to meet the demands of the twenty-first century while maintaining the gospel message and the strategic position of the church. The Summit introduces intensive seminars, workshops, and resources, addressing issues affecting the community, family, leadership, organizational health, and more.

Pastors' Wives Ministry, founded by Dr. Lois Evans, provides counsel, encouragement, and spiritual resources for pastors' wives as they serve with their husbands in ministry. The ministry focuses on the KAP Summit, which offers senior pastors' wives a safe place to reflect, renew, relax, and receive training in personal development, spiritual growth, and care for their emotional and physical well-being.

Community Impact

National Church Adopt-A-School Initiative (NCAASI) prepares churches across the country to impact communities by using public schools as the primary vehicle for effecting positive social change in urban youth and families. Leaders of churches, school districts, faith-based organizations, and other nonprofit organizations are equipped with the knowledge and tools to forge partnerships and build strong social-service delivery systems. This training is based on the comprehensive church-based community impact strategy conducted by Oak Cliff Bible Fellowship. It addresses such areas as economic development, education, housing, health revitalization, family renewal, and racial reconciliation. We also assist churches in tailoring the model to meet the specific needs of their communities while simultaneously addressing the spiritual and moral frame of reference.

Resource Development

We are fostering lifelong learning partnerships with the people we serve by providing a variety of published materials. We offer booklets, Bible studies, books, CDs, and DVDs to strengthen people in their walk with God and ministry to others.

For more information,
a catalog of Dr. Tony Evans's ministry resources,
and a complimentary copy of
Dr. Evans's devotional newsletter, call
(800) 800-3222

or write
The Urban Alternative
PO Box 4000
Dallas TX 75208

or visit our website:
www.TonyEvans.org

MORE GREAT HARVEST HOUSE BOOKS BY DR. TONY EVANS

A Moment for Your Soul

In this uplifting devotional, Dr. Evans offers a daily reading for Monday through Friday and one for the weekend—all compact, powerful, and designed to reach your deepest need. Each entry includes a relevant Scripture reading for the day.

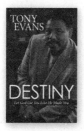

Destiny

Dr. Evans shows you the importance of finding your God-given purpose. He helps you discover and develop a custom-designed life that leads to the expansion of God's kingdom. Embracing your personal assignment from God will lead to your deepest satisfaction, God's greatest glory, and the greatest benefit to others.

The Power of God's Names

Dr. Evans shows that it's through the names of God that the nature of God is revealed. By understanding the characteristics of God as revealed through His names, you will be better equipped to face the challenges life throws at you.

Praying Through the Names of God

Dr. Evans reveals insights into some of God's powerful names and provides prayers based on those names. Your prayer life will be revitalized as you connect your needs with the relevant characteristics of His names.

Victory in Spiritual Warfare

Dr. Evans demystifies spiritual warfare and empowers you with a life-changing truth: Every struggle faced in the physical realm has its root in the spiritual realm. With passion and practicality, Dr. Evans shows you how to live a transformed life in and through the power of Christ's victory.

30 Days to Overcoming Emotional Strongholds

Dr. Evans identifies the most common and problematic emotional strongholds and demonstrates how you can break free from them—by aligning your thoughts with God's truth in the Bible.

30 Days to Victory Through Forgiveness

Has someone betrayed you? Are you suffering the consequences of your own poor choices? Or do you find yourself asking God, *Why did You let this happen?* Like a skilled physician, Dr. Evans leads you through a step-by-step remedy that will bring healing to that festering wound and get you back on your journey to your personal destiny.

Horizontal Jesus

Do you want to sense God's encouragement, comfort, and love for you every day? Dr. Evans reveals that as you live like a horizontal Jesus—giving these things away to others—you will personally experience them with God like never before.

Horizontal Jesus Study Guide

To help you live out the horizontal Jesus message, this useful study guide offers a chapter-by-chapter review of the book with Scriptures, questions to answer, and suggestions for practical application. It's great for small groups or personal study.

To learn more about Harvest House books and
to read sample chapters, visit our website:

www.harvesthousepublishers.com

HARVEST HOUSE PUBLISHERS
EUGENE, OREGON